CHAPTER ONE

I was born the fourth son of Francis Joseph and Violet Doris May Bourke on the 5th October 1931 and my given names were George Patrick. I was called George after my mother's elder brother, George Blocksidge, I never knew where the Blocksidges lived in their early days, but I can remember Uncle Jim, Mum's second brother, living with us in Princess Street, Paddington, Brisbane. It was down close to the ice works and near to the Ithaca Swimming Pool which was one of the only two that I can remember – the other one being the Valley Pool. I can remember that because Mum used to take Jimmy, my elder brother by two years, and me and drop us into the Paddington Kindergarten early in the morning and then go to work somewhere close by. Then in the afternoon Uncle Jim would pick us up, take us home and start cooking tea. Funny thing is, I can remember Uncle Jim doing that, not Pop, I suppose that's because of his job.

I can remember leaving Princess Street, a high-set house, and moving to Ada Street, Paddington, that was down behind what we called the Plaza because there was a picture show on the Tramline called "The Plaza" - our local entertainment. There and the Paddo also on the same Tramline, only closer to town.

My sister, Kathleen, born at Princess Street, was the youngest when we moved to Ada Street. I can just remember her being in the cot and Jimmy and I playing with her. It wasn't a very good place to play because the block of land behind led into a gully and Mum was always on to us - just to make sure where we were at all times. I know it wasn't a big house and it had a small verandah in the front and high at the back.

There was eight of us in this not so very big house: Mum and Pop, Uncle Jim, my elder brothers, Lesley Gordon – born 1st April 1924, Thomas Francis – born March 1926, James – born 27 August 1927, then me, and my sister, Kathleen Mary Helen – born 10th October 1933.

So Mum and Pop went and bought 48 Accession Street, Bardon, and that is where I think all our lives really started. I am not sure of the year but it would have been around 1935 or 1936 because I was around the four year mark.

I don't remember having much to do with either Les or Tommy, maybe because of the age difference, but Jimmy and Kathleen, yes.

Paddy Bourke

Came the day of the big shift to No. 48. We had to pack our few things and help to tidy up our rooms while all the biggies packed the horse and cart that Uncle Jim got from someone. I am not sure but I think Mum and Pop had a trunk of some sort. Anyway, I can remember Mum and Uncle Jim tied the load down and off we set. It was early on a Saturday and I was to go with the cart so Uncle Jim threw us up – Terry and me. He jumped up, grabbed the reins and sings out to the old bay, "Git up!"

It was something that I still remember, and always will. It was fairly hilly leading out of Ada Street, so as we took off the poor old horse was nearly off the ground! Because of the load, the shafts were lifting him in the front and he couldn't get a good grip on the ground. Uncle Jim wasn't impressed with his efforts and was going off his brain, getting up the horse and using all the profanities he could. Anyway, he was up him and we had to turn right into Amelia Street and that was steeper than Ada Street. The poor old grey was scratching and trying to pull but not good enough for Jim, who jumped off the cart and got into the horse, calling him all the lazy bastards and everything else he could think of. He was boiling so we had to jump off and get behind and "give the lazy bastard a push", he said. I don't know what he did but I can remember the horse jumping, the cart gave a jerk and two cartons fell from the back and one was full of crockery! Jim kept the bay going to the top of Amelia Street and stopped on the corner and came back. We only saved two plates – Les's and Tommy's porridge plates. They were deep set and had animals all around and in the bottom, dogs and horses, I think. The only other thing was a two tone light brown and dark brown stone made salt pot. So Jim put us back on the cart and we headed up Rockbourne Terrace and then we hit the bitumen road up the top and the tramline. Round right into Jubilee Terrace and left into Accession Street, Bardon.

That was my first real memory of our long stay at No. 48. I don't know what happened to Uncle Jim but he dropped out after that day and then Mum's older brother, George, came to stay with us. I only think that Uncle Jim must have gone off and got himself married to Aunty Phil, who turned out to be quite nice and pleasant. I can't remember her for some time to come. We all settled into No. 48 which wasn't very big. It had a small verandah on the front and off that to the left was a room which was only big enough for a single bed and small duchess – that was George's bedroom.

The verandah was closed in with brown lattice blinds and twin lattice doors. Three steps form the front then we had the main door which was typical of all the homes in those days – big and solid with a knocker on it. From there you went into a hallway, a bedroom to the left and straight opposite was the other bedroom, of the same size. So Mum and Pop took the bedroom to the left and us kids went to the right. And boy, did we have some nights in that room – must have drove Mum and Pop mad at times.

You carried on through the hallway and you had another room that they made into the dining room. Straight across was another door into the big kitchen which had a sink and the old Crown wood stove and Mum made full use of it.

I would play and fight with Jimmy and Kathleen, sometimes with Tommy, never with Les – maybe because he was a lot older but he was always around. Between him and Tommy they enjoyed teasing us younger ones, I know that brother Tommy did and Mum was always singing out to 'leave those bloody kids alone'.

I think that's all Mum ever got, "Mum, Tommy's teasing us." Poor old Tom.

STORIES FROM A SHEEP AND CATTLE MAN

The early life of Paddy Bourke, Australian bushman, drover, husband and father.

PADDY BOURKE

DEDICATION

I dedicate this book to my loving wife, Sue, the rock of my life, who has been beside me through the years – the good ones and the not so good ones ... I would be buggered without her.

    I would like to thank my daughter, Robyn, for starting me on my memoirs and without whom this book wouldn't have happened.

    Thank you also to Jennifer, my youngest daughter and to my sons Stephen, Michael and Peter, for their constant love and support.

                    Paddy Bourke

Copyright 2017 © Paddy Bourke

Paddy Bourke has asserted his right under the Copyright, Designs and Patents Act 1988 to be identified as the author.

Typed and edited by Anna Bradbury - www.annalouiselifecoaching.com
Edited, designed and published by Philip J Bradbury - www.philipjbradbury.com

ISBN- 978-0-9954398-8-7

All rights reserved. No part of this publication may be reproduced or transmitted in any form or by any means, electronic or mechanical, including photocopying, recording or any information storage and retrieval system, without permission in writing from the publisher.

I can't remember where Tommy and Les, or Jimmy for that matter, went to school. I think it might have been Ithaca Creek State School and that was a good mile away. But I can remember when I turned four and Kath was turning two, Mum said we were going to town to get our photo taken. She had bought me this red and white striped shirt with new pants and shoes – my first pair. She went to a lot of trouble dressing Kath and then got to me. She spent quite some time on me doing up my tie and hair and off we set for the tram. We caught it at what we called the Terminus – that was as far as the tram went in those days. It turned around and headed back to Stafford, Chermside and Lutwyche.

Mum was fairly light and trim in those days so walking up the two hills wasn't that hard for her in the early years but they became harder some years down the track. We got the tram and headed into George Street in the city. We kids were free and it cost Mum a penny.

I can recall we got off at Roma Street because that was a section stop. Any further and you paid another penny. We walked up George Street, Mum carrying Kath and we called into the Lyceum Theatre as the lady who owned it was a friend of Pop's, a Mrs Lloyd. Then we went back two doors and upstairs to the Studio where this man spent a lot of time on me because I had a turned left eye and he wanted to get it right – which he did eventually.

I don't know what Mum paid for the two portraits but they were big ones and we both still have them to this day. So every time I look at mine, I think of Mum and the trouble she went to on that day. That's my second biggest day as a child.

Mum still used to go to work as a cleaning and washing and ironing lady, as we knew her. Then came the big day when she took me to school. Because Kathleen was so young we got a cab. Mr Hutchinson, who lived just behind us in Carmel Street, had a blue and white cab. There were only two cab companies in those days – blue and white, and black and white.

We went to St Finbars, a Catholic school run by the Saint Franciscans. In those days it was roughly a mile away or better – a fair walk but we did it and in bare feet as there wasn't too many kids who had shoes then. I did like going to school as the teacher I had was a lovely woman or nun and her name was Mother Jarlet. She was the head nun and any others under her were called 'sisters'. I would have been around four and a half to five years old as I was in the prep grade.

I finished that term and I can remember taking Mum home a note saying that there was going to be another convent starting up and every kid living on the west side of Ithaca Creek had to go to the new school called St Joseph's – run by the nuns. One that you could never forget was Mother Patricia. What a terrible, savage and cruel bitch she was. When I look back and think of her, they are not good memories. Father Healey and Father Lyons, came later. Father Healey was the elderly one and was the big boss of them all. He had a nice way and manner and, in my opinion - one shared by all of us some years later, serviced the nuns in more ways than you would like to think of. Mother Patricia would have been last and the only pleasure Healey would want from her, would have been to roll her on her gut and go from there. That's why she was so bitter and twisted.

It was around 1938 when we all first went to St Joseph's. There were only a few of us then. Mum sent Tommy, Jimmy and me. First they had no school house so the big kids used to learn in the old church, just inside to the right of the main gate and all us younger ones were over at what they called the 'Nunnery'. That's where all the nuns used to live and eat. The nuns sectioned off the side verandah and that's where we were taught.

It started off small but as the years went by, more and more kids came. The nuns used to get all the kids to clean the rooms out and the toilets, which was the old thunderbox. We would clean all around the nunnery and some Fridays we would have to stack all the desks and stools that we had used through the week to the back of the church. Then bring all of the pews and set them out so as they would be ready for Benediction on the Friday night.

One thing about the nuns that you would always find is that they were either in a good mood or a really bad one. One day, early in the morning, Mother Patricia was called to the phone inside. She gave us some work to do and said in her savage way that we were not to talk in class while she was away. As soon as she left the room, we all started talking and mucking around. She was away for quite some time and boy, when she came into the room, didn't she go off. She lined the whole class up and started to give everyone the cane. One hit on the hand for the girls and two hits for the boys. My mate, Raymond Cross, and me stayed in our seats and when it was all over and everyone was sitting down, nearly all the girls were crying and some of the boys.

Out of the blue one of the girls said out loud, "It's not fair, Paddy Bourke and Ray Cross didn't get the cane."

Well, the savage old bitch looked straight at us and said out loud, "Bourke, Cross, get here now." Which we did and didn't she give it to us – but it never killed us.

I can recall the Sunday when Franky, Kath and me went to church. We were up front, three pews back and the hall was full. They passed the plate around and a lot of people put small packets on the plate. Others just put coins on it. We used to just pass it as we never had any money.

I got this bright idea and I said to the others, "Come on, we will leave early." So just before the end we walked out.

Now the old nuns were watching and we knew what would happen on Monday – they would stand up in front of the class and give you a dressing down for leaving early. We took off and when we got to the hallway at the front where they used to leave the plates on a small table with all the loose money and small packets, I took a packet and we were off and up the road. We opened it up and there was 2s 6d which was a lot of money to us in those days. Franky, and more so Kathleen, were panicking and wanted to put it back but me being the eldest said, "No. Come on, we will go for a tram ride."

And that we did, all the way out to Chermside which was a new line just opened up. We got ice cream and lollies and still had money left over.

It was a month or two later that my conscience got the better of me, so one Sunday morning I went to Confession and Father Lyons, the younger of the Priests, was in the box - he was the hardest of the two. He was sitting there bored shitless, until I got to the front where I said, "Father, I took a packet from the plate."

He sat straight up and he was a tall man. I could see him looking straight at me and the first thing he said was, "You what? How much was in it?"

I told him it was 2s 6d and what I had done with it. Then he gave me my penance and if I had said all the prayers I think I would have been still there!

Back at No. 48 where everything used to happen, I was about seven years old when one Saturday this mob of boys was shifting into No. 50 on the bottom side of No. 48. We were running and playing and this blonde fellow my size came up and wanted to know my name and age and I asked the same. That was the start of our friendship that lasted until he died in early 1999. His name, he told me, was Bernie Briggs and he was six years old.

By this time there were seven kids at No. 48 – six boys and one girl. At No. 50 there were six boys and Bernie was number three. Then out of the blue on the top side, another mob moved in. They were the Leeds family of four – three girls and one boy. They ended up a total of six. We ended up ten, the Briggs nine. So between the three homes there were 25 kids and, apart from a lot of arguing and disagreement, we got on pretty good.

Immediately behind us in Carmel Street was a family of five boys, the Cheringtons and we never got on real good with them. Their father killed our dog, a red kelpie we called Jock. He split his head with an iron bar so whenever we had a reason, we would get up them.

One day I will never forget, Mum and Pop weren't at home and we ended up having a stone fight – Briggs and Bourkes against the Cheringntons. We were throwing anything and everything at them, even the peaches and apricots off our tree, when someone sang out that we were out of stones. I said I knew there were more in the sideboard so we all raced upstairs. Pop had a biscuit tin and in it was a canvas bag with all these big, blue metal rocks with some streaks of yellow through them all. We all raced back down and started the war again. As we would throw down at them they would pick up the same ammo and throw it back at us. I saw Franky Cherington throw his stone and it came straight at me and I couldn't get out of the way. It hit me on the forehead and blood went everywhere. Mum was home by then so she called the ambulance which took me to the Brisbane Children's Hospital. I ended up with three stiches – one of many sets of stitches I was to end up with.

It was quite some time after that fight (one of many) that Pop went to the sideboard and to the tin and found all the rocks missing. He asked the big ones who took them and they blamed me. I was downstairs playing when all hell broke loose. Pop was that mad – I had never seen him madder. He belted the shit out of me with his razor strap.

He was yelling at me and I was screaming out and crying when out of the blue came Uncle George and he said, "Alright Frank, leave the bloody kid alone. He's had enough."

Pop said, "I'll kill the young bastard."

So Uncle George took me up to his room at the front of the house and I locked myself in. Sometime later Kath came and told me that dinner was ready and I asked her if Pop was there. She told me a lie and said no. So I jumped out the front window, up the back steps and into the kitchen. I bloody nearly died – Pop was sitting in his chair at the top of the big table. Everybody else was there too.

I was about to bolt and Mum said, "You sit there." And she sat me in Uncle's chair as he had shifted down one. So there we were, Pop at one end, me at the other and the whole mob all quiet.

I kept on looking at Pop with my head down and looking up he said, "I'll give you looking at me under your bloody eyelids."

Mum told him to have his dinner and to leave me alone which he did, thank God. He bought it up many, many years later in the Lennons Motel in George Street. We were having a beer and he said, "You threw a lot of money away that day. Those rocks had a lot of gold in them."

He had gone to get the rocks to get the gold out of them which was when he found them missing. So I always told my kids that one day they would read where someone had found gold at Bardon. That hiding I got for throwing away Pop's gold was the worst but only one of many. I have always said they never really hurt me and they certainly didn't do me any harm. But we all kept Pop in practice with his strap!

I can remember Christmas 1938 or 1939. I was seven and Mum bought us a scooter - rubber tyred and two tone pink colour, which was for all of us. We were told not to take it out till later. While they were having dinner I sneaked it out from the front verandah and raced up to the top of Accession Street – they were all dirt roads in those days, rough too with little gullies through them from the rain.

A Mr Robinson was on his way home from work and he was nearly down the bottom of the hill when I sang out to him, "Hey, Mr Robinson, you watch me."

He sang out, "Right oh. You be careful."

So I let it go flat out, hanging on like buggery. I got nearly to the bottom when I hit the steel cap of the water main – which is still there today. The scooter was held together by a cotton pin holding the handle bars and front wheel to the step and back wheel. When I hit the steel cap the pin jumped out, the scooter split in half and went flying. I left the scooter and ran home screaming (that always seemed the thing to do!). Poor old Mum did the usual and came running. She carried me to the kitchen and put me on the big table and said to one of the big ones to run up to Maggie's and call the ambulance. When they got to our home, and they all knew how to get to Accession Street, they came in and started to patch me up.

The ambo man looked at me and said, "You can sing out if you want."

He was sorry he said that to me because when he got to my right kneecap (which was a mess) he started to clean it up and I started yelling and screaming. He took one look at me and said, "Hey, I didn't mean that loud!"

So off to Brisbane Children's Hospital (B.C.H.) where they admitted me that night. I woke in the morning and the sister was dressing my hands. She said, "You're not going to yell are you?"

I said, "No."

She asked me, "Would you hold the torch for me?"

That I did and I watched as she pulled out all the finger nails, except the thumb, on my left hand. They stitched my kneecap up and fixed all the other cuts up and I was out within a week. I can remember it well because I got my name on the front page of the Courier Mail - Mum kept the column.

Pop came up to see me in the ward and said, "I'll throw that bloody scooter away when I get home." But when I got home, there it was. Poor old Pop.

Then there was the time, early in the move to No. 48, our first Christmas when I was around four or five. Mum got me this wooden trumpet. It was solid and about six inches long and had a split mouthpiece. I was running around everywhere, blowing this bloody noisy thing, as Mum called it. Mum was talking to her new neighbour, a big woman. I was sucking and blowing when, all of a sudden, I sucked too hard and the tin whistle came out and got stuck in my throat. I couldn't talk or sing out and, when Mum turned around and saw me, she panicked and this other lady sang out to her, "Tip him up!"

By this time, with me choking and going on, Mum panicking, this lady got through the old paling fence, picked me up with one arm and thumped the hell out of my back. It did the job, but in reverse - instead of coughing it up, I swallowed it. So it was, again, call the ambos and off to the B.C.H. - O'Connell Ward I used to go to. I was there for nearly a week and they fed me all this soft tucker – porridge and puddings – and, unknown to me, they had cotton wool mixed up in it. They called Mum up to take me home and I can still recall the whistle hanging up on the light cord over the sister's desk. They told Mum that if I hadn't passed it with cotton wool, it would have been a big operation. So I was lucky.

Then there was this cold Sunday morning and Tommy and me were up early. Tommy said, "Come on, we'll make Mum and Pop a cuppa."

So we got out the small primus stove which stood on three legs and had a small container for the methylated spirits. This always boiled the tin kettle quickly - Pop did it all the time. Well, the kettle was just off the boil and Tommy said it needs more metho. He thought that the flame had gone out but it hadn't and we didn't know it. I was standing opposite him so when he tipped the bottle to pour into the small primus, all hell broke loose. The meths caught on fire and it sprayed all over me and my pyjamas. I stood and tried to brush the fire away from my face. When I couldn't do that, I took off, running through the house, me screaming and Tommy yelling out to stop. Out the front, back down beside Mum's room, and that was one place we never went near because Pop used to spit out the window and he used to aim for the wattle tree in Leeds' yard. Good aim too.

Tommy and I were still running and I was going in and out around all the stumps under the house. Tommy couldn't catch me and he did the only thing he could at the time – he turned the hose on me. Just as the water hit me, I stopped. Then the whole house was alive. Mum wrapped a blanket round me, Pop carried me upstairs and all I can remember was the old calling again – "Call the ambos" – and off I went to the B.C.H. and to O'Connell Ward again. That was the first time I was in an ambulance with the sirens going. I was not quite twelve years and I could hear them arguing on the two-way which way to take me. Because I was going to be in for a while they decided on the Brisbane General, Ward, 2A. What a day!

I can remember Pop coming in to the ward, after they had me settled and sedated, and saying, once again, "The bloody primus. I'll chuck it in the shit house when I get home."

Nearly three months later, when I got home, the primus was still sitting there. Poor old Pop.

I got used to the nurses and the ward, I knew all the patients by their names so that when Mum came to take me home, I didn't want to go and, when I got home, I got home-sick for the hospital. They really looked after you in those days.

I was an out-patient for a while. I had to go from Bardon by tram to the B.G.H. two or three times a week and, when I got better, they broke the visits down. I found it very uncomfortable and hard to put up with because I was bandaged from the waist down to below the calf. The treatment used to hurt like hell. I had to stand on my left leg and kick my hip outward. The nurse would freeze my leg and then the doctor would get this small but very sharp knife and cut all the extra flesh off my leg. Then they would put blue stone powder all over the cut flesh and bandage me up and off I would go back home. I would get as far as the tram stop at the exhibition grounds and that's where I would sit and cry with pain until I could get on the tram. But what I went through then was nothing.

When I came off that scooter I was around seven years old and, while I was in O'Connell Ward for kids, I met Colin McCloud who was in for burns treatment. I got to know him because we played together. When I got over the worst of my burns, they took me from inside the ward and put me out on the verandah. Well, the first bloke I saw was this Colin and he was still in hospital for the same burns that he had five years ago. So I was a lot better off than he was and, between the two of us, we sure kept those poor nurses busy!

I don't know how it came about but I left St Joseph's Convent and went to Ithaca State School with Jimmy and Tom. Les was already going there, if I remember right. The convent could only teach up to first grade. Then you had to go to the big school as classes only went to seventh grade. Then, if you wanted, you did the big one which was what they called Scholarship. Bernie talked me into going to Ashgrove State and, once I was there for a while, Jimmy came over too. So Mum had three schools – Tom and Les to Ithaca, Jimmy and me to Ashgrove and Kathleen still at convent.

CHAPTER TWO

I can still remember the very first day I played the wag. It was a Wednesday and Jimmy says, "We don't go." We all stayed down at what they called the flats – there were dairies everywhere in those days. Joe Todd, Olivers and Gramendes, all had their dairies along the creek. They had a lot of corn fields and paddocks, roughly about five to ten acres, not too many houses. So we used to play along the creek and in the corn paddock. When we got in the corn, someone must have phoned the dairies – mostly Teddy's – and up he would come and sing out, "Hey you kids! Get out of that corn."

We would hide wouldn't we! So, after a while he would go and, if we stayed, he would send his man, Porky Rollo, up on a horse and he would chase us until we got out and headed back for the creek. This would go on for as long as we wanted and I'm sure we drove Teddy and Porky mad.

That first day playing wag was one of the worst things that happened to me as it was not compulsory to go to school because of the war. I found that I didn't want to go and I hardly ever did after that. However, poor Hackey Briggs' father found out about him and he got a flogging with the ironing cord. I can remember him coming over home to borrow the bottle of milk, cup of sugar or whatever, and we used to do the same. He pulled his shirt up and showed Mum and he was black and blue from the hiding. He would never play the wag again and neither would Bernie.

Jimmy turned 14 years and that's when you could leave school; which he did and he had to get a job. I can remember Manpower, something to do with the government. came chasing him when he left his job and they had him back working straight away.

I had to go to school on my own and didn't like it. That was when I really started to wag it. I used to go on the milk run with Teddy Lisk – his father had the dairy down the bottom of the street. They were in Coronation Street and old Mr Lisk milked around 30 odd cows and everything was done by hand. Jimmy and I would go over quite a lot and give Billy Lisk a hand to mix the feed, put the feed into four gallon kerosene tins with the top cut out and the sides bent over so it wouldn't cut you. We would carry four tins at the one time, from the feed shed to the milking bails twice every day. We would cut the corn with a big reaping hook then cut it up in the chaff cutter by hand – hard work but we thought nothing of it. After we finished the milk run, all done on foot, I would go back home and go through the act of going to school.

I would, instead, head for the plaza area and meet up with George Lewis and he would pay me 5/- a week to help him on the ice run. That was hard till you got used to it, carrying those cold ice blocks for the ice chest and nearly every house had an ice chest. You would race in, sing out loud, "Iceman!" and they would take you through to the ice chest and you had to place the blocks in the chest for them.

If I didn't want to do the run I could and would go on the butchers run and that was all done with the cane basket the same as the bread run. I would get paid every day I went and that's how I could go to town nearly any time or day that I didn't go to school.

Then Sergeant Osborne from Ashgrove got on to me for wagging it and he was forever chasing me on his motor bike and side car. I know I was a pain in his arse because, when he did catch up with me, he would be very cranky. One day, after picking me up from home, he took me to the station and started to ask me where I had been every time.

He would say, "Where were you Monday?"

I would say, "I don't know," or "I forget" and, after a while he snapped.

He said, "I'll make you bloody remember," and pulled off his big belt. He gave me two or more cracks across the arse and, all of a sudden, my memory came back to me and I told him where I had been. Then came the time to go to school. I was that used to him picking me up from wherever and taking me straight to the school and dropping me off right at the front door of Ashgrove State and all of the kids would give me heaps.

This morning I ran outside where he had his side car. I jumped in and waited for him to come. I would say he was watching me because he came out from the station, stood beside me and looked.

He said, "What do you think you're doing?"

I said, "Going to school, sir."

He said, "I know you are but you're running. Get out. Now, I know I can't catch you, Paddy, and if you run from me you will be a sorry boy so don't you try it."

Believe me, I could tell by his voice that he meant it so he rode beside me all along the Ashgrove tram line saying so as everybody could hear him, "Come on, faster!". There were a lot of people waiting to catch the trams, going to work and I could see and feel them watching me. But even that didn't stop me from wagging it.

This period in my school days started before I got burnt so, when I was in hospital I sure didn't miss school. I was off with the burns well over six months so when I was finally discharged, I definitely didn't want to go back to school.

Mum took me back and I had to go to the headmaster's room, a Mr McComb, a real nice man – very firm but good. He took me to my new classroom and a Miss Latimer was to be my new teacher. The class was in and Mr McComb introduced me to them and then he told them that, because I had missed so much schooling from my accident – I am sure he would have liked to have said wagging it too but didn't – that I was to be put down a class. But, if I could prove myself, he would put me back into my original class. So I really felt out of place and definitely didn't want to go to school.

They tried everything on me. I had a book that Mum had to sign when I left home, then by my teacher when I got to school, and the same in reverse when I left school and when I got home.

Bernie and I were selling newspapers for the Felix Paper and Casket Shop, right next to the Transcontinental Hotel, Roma Street, and we were making good money getting 2s 6d a dozen and we would sell nothing under two dozen and more each and every afternoon.

But we would also get lots of tips. Sometimes we would have 1/- or more in tips and this we kept a good count on. We would tell Miss Zoey and then she started keeping our tips, saying that we were so much short. We knew we weren't short at all and it turned out her loss. She got new books and magazines in every Friday so, come Saturday morning, we would get in early and be waiting for the papers and Bernie got the idea to knock off some comics – all the go in those days - 6d each.

He would get up one end of the book stand and me at the other end and he would say, "This is a good one here. You see this." If I said yes, that meant for him to take it and I would do the same down my end. We would put the book down our shirt front. We had asked Miss Zoey if we could read while we were waiting and she said, "Yes but don't tear or get them dirty."

So we did all of this knocking off right in front of her. When we got enough books we would walk round to the front of the Transcontinental and I would set up our own little book stand with a fruit box. If she wanted to, she could have seen us. We had a lot of regulars and we were selling them cheaper than the shop so we made up for our tips that way, after her taking our tips like she did. We would take our money out of the money bag and she could do it all on her own. The old bitch never did wake up to what we did to her.

The only reason I left was because Bernie came running up to me one Saturday night and said, "Quick, your Pop's coming!" So I gave him my papers and money. If Pop had caught me selling papers he would have got into me on the spot and I didn't want that.

Jimmy, Billy Lisk and me went shoe shining in Queen Street once – two bob a shine. There were a lot of yanks about in those days and they would always tip you if you did a good shine. Anyway, we were chipped into the police. One came off point duty from the corner of Creek and Queen Street and told us we had to have a hawker's license.

So we just moved up the road a-piece and we were doing alright when, all of a sudden, I said, "Here comes Pop!"

You could pick him out a mile as he was so tall. We grabbed all the gear – two fruit cases, one to sit on and one to put their shoe on while you polished it. We grabbed that and we ran up Queen Street and threw the boxes down a laneway. There were a lot of people around and you should have seen them jump when Jimmy and Billy chucked the boxes. That was the finish of our shoe shining.

This all happened while we should have been at school so that's why we ran when Pop was around. We were never caught but he was stout and firm and when he told us to do something, we did it. When he was on the go and was going to belt anyone of us you would always see Mum racing around the house hiding all the straps, Pop's sandshoes, sewing machine cord and anything else he might use.

I remember early in the time we moved to No. 48, old Jenks the Sergeant from the Terminus, as we called it, came down and told Pop that us kids had robbed the church on Jubilee Terrace just up the road. So Pop got Les and Tommy in the bedroom and belted the shit out of them both. I was in my cot ready for bed and I was screaming as loud as my brothers. Mum was yelling to him to stop and banging on the door as he had it locked.

When he has finished with them, all he did was walk past me, pat my head and said, "Now for that little bastard in the kitchen."

That was Jimmy – who didn't wait around. He jumped out the kitchen window, about a 10 foot drop, and took off. I think Pop got him a day or so later but the best part was to come. Jenks the cop (who wasn't rapt in the Bourkes, Briggs, Lisks, and Cocks families - all big ones) came down one afternoon and Pop had to get out of bed as he was on night shift and was in bed asleep. Mum went and told him that Jenks was here. When Pop came out he wasn't happy to see him – he didn't like the police coming to his door. Jenks said he was sorry but his kids didn't do the robbery of the church and was sorry if he caused any trouble. Well, Pop flew up and told him to get the buggery off his verandah. Jenks was also tall but heavier than Pop but if he hadn't gone I am sure Pop would have got into the big bludger.

Jenks knocked his cap off at the door, picked it up and when he finished slamming the gate, turned to Pop and said, "Alright Frank, you keep your kids off the street because if you don't, I will." And from that day on he had every one of us on his list.

The Moores lived over the road from us and I used to play with Joe. He was a year younger than me. They were a nice family and kept to themselves. Joe had a lot of good pigeons, all colours and breeds, and we used to go into Roma Street where the fruit markets were in those days. It was overrun with all sorts of birds but mainly pigeons. We would go in and catch what we wanted, take them home, feed them for some period of time, then we would let them out for a run and they would go straight back to Roma Street. So every now and again we would sneak over to the Moore's place in the night and pinch some of Joe's but they were homing pigeons and as soon as we let them out, they also would go straight back to Joe's. If he missed his birds he would come over to our place, let his go and take some of ours. That went on for a long time.

When I was about 12, Mum bought a nice looking grey mare – a trotter. Then she bought this nice sulky which she drove all around Brisbane and always to Albion Racetrack on the Saturdays. She would tie her up with a feed bag and meet Pop inside and sometimes she would bring him home. She used to take old Maggie Smith and Kathleen with her. A lot of police on point duty got to know her and used to give her the right of way. A lot of the Bardon tram drivers knew her and sometimes used to race Mum on the way home and old Floss knew it too. Then she bought this little black pony stallion and gave him to me.

I thought it was great and I used to do all sorts of tricks on him. Then I started riding him to school and I used to let him loose in the church yard at the Ashgrove Tram Terminus. Just across the road was the school and if anyone gave me a hard time through the day, I used to hurry over to Tony, that was his name, slip the bridle on him then go looking for whoever I was after. I would chase them until they either ran back to the school yard or jumped somebody's fence. I did that for some time until someone told Mum and she stopped me from riding him to school.

I was riding him up the Terminus one day and my brother Tommy was there. I was showing off and was showing him how I could gallop under the trees and grab a branch and land on the ground. And I could do it but something went wrong this day. Tommy was going to test me and I missed the branch and hit the ground hard and broke my right wrist. I got up crying. Tommy came over and like always, started to put the wind up me saying that my hand was going to be fall off and that we better hurry home. So I jumped on the horse and got home in a hurry. Next thing the ambulance was there and they took me with Mum to B.C.H. They x-rayed it and then put me in a cubicle and every so often a nurse would come in and ask me how I was feeling, and how long was it since I ate, and I would tell and they would say, "You'll be right. You just lay there."

I started to wonder where Mum was. She did tell me that she was going to visit Leedsy, our neighbour, and that she wouldn't be long but that was hours ago.

Then a Senior Sister came to me and said, "You're the young fellow with the broken wrist. Don't you go away because they are going to operate on you in a minute." And she gave me a pat and left.

As soon as she said that word 'operate' I packed the jimmy shits. So when she left I grabbed my splints and bandages that the ambulance man had put on me and put them inside my shirt. I started to walk out and Sister saw me and asked, "Where are you going?"

I said, "To the toilet."

She said, "Well, don't you be long, they are going to fix that arm of yours now."

So I did go to the toilet, where I wrapped my arm up the best I could and then I took off out the front gate and ran home to No. 48. Poor old Mum got home late and was cranky. I heard her telling Pop that they had everybody out looking for me – all the nurses and staff, the wardsmen and security. So they said nothing to me and I went to bed in pain but Mum gave me a bexpowder and that put me to sleep.

The next morning Pop came and woke me up. Never said much (never did), just "Get up and have a shower." Which I did.

Then I went to eat my Vita Brits and he says, "Nothing for you. We have to hurry and leave."

So up we go to the Terminus and we get an early tram and I heard him say 1 ½ to the hospital and I really got scared but I wasn't game to take on Pop – he could run pretty good in his day. When we walked in, the Sister who saw me yesterday was the first to see me and said to everyone, "Hey, this is the young one who took off and did a bunk on us yesterday."

So she thanked Pop and told him to wait outside. She said to me to come with her and took me straight to a table and laid me down. I would say in less than a minute a doctor was there putting the mask over my mouth and nose and said to me, "Count back from ten."

It happened that fast and they were all over me, holding me down that I didn't have time to think. I woke up and the old man was sitting there with his big grin and all he did was chuckle. That was my first break. It didn't stop me from riding Tony as I only had the plaster on my arm up to the elbow.

It was just after I got my arm out of plaster that Kath and I were up the Terminus getting the daily milk and bread when I saw this army man get off the tram. He had his big bag and his haversack on his back and when we saw him we got all excited. It was our oldest brother, Les, home from the war. He had been away for 18 months or more and was on leave. Nobody knew he was coming so I grabbed his khaki haversack and with the milk, I took off.

It's a day I'll never forget. Mum was talking to Mrs Briggs down the side of the house and I rushed in singing out, "Look what I found!"

As soon as she saw the bag she took off running and crying and she met Les and Kath up the road. That was unreal. Les was the centre of attention that night. Pop came home from work and there was a tear in his eye. After tea we all sat round the big kitchen table listening to what he said. He was to have forty days leave he told Mum, and, as the days went by, we all got used to him coming and going. He brought home one of his mates – a Bobby Shaw – who came from Melbourne. We all liked him.

Then one day he came home and told Mum that they had to go back to the islands. That was half-way through the war when things didn't look so good. Came the night when he said they were leaving and we all said our goodbyes. Mum was crying and a lot of us young ones were too, and away he went on his own back to Enoggera Barracks. He was to sail that night, he said. The next day he was back home and kept on saying that was for a good week or more. Then, one day, he said his goodbyes and we never saw him again for another two and a half years.

When he finally came home the war was over. No one knew he was coming home. Kelly, the army chap living with Mrs Leeds next door, was in town and saw all the army boys marching through the town from the wharves and they broke up on Roma Street. Kelly told Mrs Leeds that he would put money on it that he saw Les and sure as hell, he came home on the tram again. He was discharged some time later and that's when he had a bad time with malaria and nightmares.

Les went back working with his old firm, Plumeridges Lolly, a factory in Barry Parade in Fortitude Valley, next to the Nestles factory. Les was with them for years and, like a lot of other places, they had to give the returned soldiers their jobs back when they came back and they didn't like it. Les had a falling-out, left and went with the Post Master General, and was with them until he retired many years later.

By the time the war was over and we were still at No. 48, there was another five kids born. Mum had all the babies, from Franky down to Margaret the youngest, in their bedroom. There was this midwife, Sister Richards, a lovely woman. She lived up at the Terminus, just near and across the road from the police station. Every time Mum was due to have a baby, Pop used to get one of us to tell Mrs Richards, "Mum wants you in a hurry!"

She would come straight away and stay until everything was right. She used to get Pop to keep the fire going and keep the kettle on. The only baby Mum had at Brisbane General Hospital was the last time, a girl, but she died at birth. They kept Mum for quite some time. I used to go up and see her and I would sing out to her from downstairs as I knew she slept on the verandah. I heard her telling Mrs Leeds that all the other women would make a joke of it and say there's your Romeo downstairs. We were all glad to see her home again.

By the time 1943 came along we were still in the middle of WWII and there was Mum and Pop and they now had 10 kids, nine living at home and Les still away at war. So No. 48 was full. There were nine boys and one girl in the middle of them all. Next door at No. 50 were the Briggs and the Briggs and the Bourkes were the largest families around. A lot of seven and eight children but not 10. We all got on pretty good, had our fights and squabbles but always ended up friends.

Bernie and I always paired off. He got a job after school working in a corner store on the Ashgrove tram line. I would go home and get my horse and canter over to the shop and when I got near to the front, I would make Tony bounce around and make a noise on the bitumen. That was the sign to Bernie that I was waiting for him around the corner where there was a window and he would throw out bickies, lollies and cigarettes. I would jump the fence, stuff them down my shirt and canter off back to our hideout that was down the bottom of Accession and Coronation Streets. We would hide it in the thick lantana, sell the cigs and eat all the rest. He left the corner shop after some time and got a job in the big shop at the Ashgrove Tram Terminus just around the corner from school - that was good to us too. The bit that we took from the shops, they got back in our labour, so we didn't feel guilty.

Raymond Cross, who I went to the Convent with, lived just up the road on Empress Terrace. He and I got into a lot of strife, not bad, but bad enough. Pop didn't like me hanging around with him so I had to sneak around to his place. He had a big black dog called Nigger who would go for anyone who came near us.

Our favourite pastime while wagging would be to pick on the telegram boys while they were riding their bikes around delivering telegrams. We would grab their bikes while they were inside somebody's house and ride it up the road. They would see us and start chasing us and when they got too close, we would jump off and sing out for Nigger. He would really frighten them but never hurt them. They all got to know us and the Postmaster reported us to Jenks, the Sergeant. He would have liked to have caught us but didn't.

One day I ended up at Ray's house and it was dark and he talked me into staying at his place. So I snuck up the front stairs, about 20 of them, and I got under his bed. He started throwing some blankets and coats to me and his mother saw him and said, "What are you doing, Ray?"

He said, "Making a bed for Nigger, Mum."

I went to sleep and the next thing I hear Jenks at the front door and Ray's father was talking to him. He asked if they had seen me and if Ray was in bed. He said no, and that Ray was in bed and showed him as the bed was right at the door. Jenks said if he saw me to let him know.

When they left, Ray whispered, "Did you hear that?"

I said, "Yes, I hope he don't come back."

I could see Mr Cross in the lounge room sitting there reading and smoking his pipe. It was pretty late and I heard him lighting his pipe when he dropped his matches. He bent down to pick them up and as he did, he looked under the bed and saw me. He started singing out to everyone, "Here he is. Quick, call Jenks."

And that they did. Jenks came down, got me, took me to the station and gave me a rousing. He threatened me with Westbrook (Farm for Boys), then took me home in his big Humber car. I knew Mum wouldn't say anything but I was frightened of Pop. But it turned out Pop was on night shift so all I got was a warning from Mum and tucked into bed.

CHAPTER THREE

After I got over my burns and was back at school, Jimmy was already working. The Briggs wouldn't wag with me and I didn't blame them as their father wasn't the nicest man and he really flogged them when he took to them. I was on my own and definitely didn't want to go to school and I was driving old Sergeant Osborne mad. He used to even try and catch me at home, morning or night. One day he coasted down the hill near Liskys Dairy. I was on my way out for the day looking after the milking cows, about 40 all up, and there he was, looking straight at me.

All he said was, "Don't you run Paddy. Come here. Why aren't you at school?"

"Mum said I could have the day off, sir."

And then he said, "Did she eh? Well, get in and we'll go and have a talk to her."

He took me home and Mum came to the front door and was talking to him softly. He must have guessed and asked if Mr Bourke was at home.

Mum said, "Yes, but he's on night shift and I don't want to wake him."

Well, Pop must have woke and heard them. Next thing he was standing beside me and asked the Sergeant what was wrong. When Sergeant Osborne, who I liked and had a lot of respect for, told Pop my pedigree and how long it had been going for, I could hear Pop stirring.

"So Mr Bourke, I will leave him with you and will return in half an hour and take him to school again." And he left.

Well, Pop put me in the bedroom and went and got his big razor strap. Mum didn't have time to do what she always did in these times and that was hide anything Pop could belt you with. When he came in and started, I did the usual yell as loud as I could and race around the room. He would chase me all over, under the bed, around the bed. Mum did the norm, got in the door and stopped him, "Leave him alone, he's had enough."

Said Pop, "I'll kill the young bastard." And I thought he was trying to.

Mum got me cleaned up and I was reading and waiting for the Sergeant. He was back in half an hour and he told me to wait in the side car. He had a talk with Mum and Pop and then we were off to school.

What I didn't know was that when the war finished it became compulsory to go to school and that was why he hadn't forced me to go to school before. So on the way he was driving slow and I always remember what he said to me word for word.

We were going along the flats near the corn fields and he was leaning over towards me and he said, "Paddy, we bloody well have had you. I've had a gut full of you. Only for your mother and father having a big family I would have put you into Westbrook a long time ago. So when you go home today you have a talk to them and work something out because if you don't go to school from today on, that's where you will be going."

I really knew that he meant it and you always did what he said. He drove me right to the front door, gave me his little salute and said, "Good luck Paddy." And that was the last time I ever saw Sergeant Osborne.

Mr McCombe, the headmaster, took me to his room and had a talk to me but I wasn't interested in what he said and don't remember any of it like I did, and still do, with the Sergeant.

That night Mum and Pop had a talk to me and said that they were going to send me to a college for boys up at Mt Tambourine and would I like that. I said yes, not realising what I was going into.

Come the weekend Mum had a port[1] of clothes packed for me. I had my first pair of good black shoes and a pair of sandshoes. I can remember it being a Sunday. I said goodbye to Mum, who was crying and telling me to look after myself, not to get into any trouble and to behave myself. Pop carried my port and we caught the tram into Roma Street. Then a train to Beenleigh and then a bus to Mt Tambourine. Eagle Heights was where the college was on both sides of the road.

We didn't talk much, Pop never did. I suppose he was thinking of how they were going to pay the loan back. Being so young I never understood or realized how much pressure I had put on them. I found out quite some years down the track that my Aunty Elsie, who was Pop's eldest sister, had paid to put me into college and it cost a lot. They had to outfit me with the clothes that the Brothers wanted – I even got my first suit and shoes. Plus she paid for my lodging.

We got to the school after dinner. Pop took me in and met the Head Brother. I don't remember any of their names. He only stayed for a short time as he had to catch the same bus back. He rubbed me on the head, said pretty much the same as Mum, and he was gone.

I was in the hands of the devil. The Head Brother took me around and introduced me to all the other Brothers and some of the boys who I would be in school with. Then he took me to a nice room. It was in the main house – all the Brothers and staff stayed there.

He said, "We'll put you in here until you settle in and then we will put you in the main dormitory." And he gave me all the dos and don'ts.

As soon as he left me on my own, that's when it hit me and I knew my life had, and would, change from that day and it sure as hell did. They gave me a good week to settle in and that I did. The boys were alright and I fitted in with them. The Brothers put me in the football team and I played full back. Then they said they would change me to the wing as I was a good runner – I liked that. Saturday mornings was gymnastics. I

---

1   Port is a suitcase

could do everything on the vaulting horse bar – the full somersault and there was only one other boy who could do it. I was to get to know him some time later.

I found the Brothers had two different personalities The first was while you were out of school and in the yard etc - they were real friendly. They would mix and play, show you things, do anything for you. And the second was when we had to go back inside after the bell and then they became very strict and stood no nonsense.

There was one day that I had a fall out with one of the bigger boys down the road near the little shop. We were punching up like boys do and the Brothers caught us, soused on us and sent us back to the gym. They made us put gloves on, get in the ring and punch it out. One brother was in the ring with us refereeing and when we had enough he said, "That's it. And I don't want to see any more arguing on the grounds again. If I catch either of you again, look out. Understand!"

"Yes, sir." We said.

The tone and look of him was enough. The boy I fought was Bill Doubting and we finished up good mates.

They gave me a job to do - I was to sweep the dormitory out every morning. The day started at 6 am when the Brother would come in, stand at the door and look about. If a bed was empty, he would wait for a while then walk to the toilets and check that the boy was there. Then he would walk up one isle and down the other, then stand at the door he came in and clap his hands real loud and in a clear voice say, "Good morning boys."

You were to jump out of bed, say a quick prayer, go to the toilet, have a wash, comb your hair, come back, get dressed, then make your bed and stand there. The Brother who was walking around talking and watching all the time, he would come to you and inspect your bed then your dress and if anything wasn't right he would tell you so as everyone else could hear, and make you do it right. Then you would have to wait for another inspection and if that wasn't right, look out – punishment time.

Then you would go downstairs and play and wait for the bell to ring. First one was church, then outside and wait for the second bell – that was breakfast. You had the same table, same place. Start eating and no talking or mucking around. Where ever you went and whatever you did there was always a Brother watching and supervising. I always reckoned it was to see no boy did a bunk.

One time I got caught mucking around at the meal table. The Brother called me out, "Front and center Bourke."

I shit myself, so out I go and in front of the whole school, he dresses me down and says, "You sit out here until I tell you different." And he pointed to a big table where about eight boys were having their meal. He was standing only feet away from them and where he stood, he could see every table.

So my next meal I was moved to what they called The Rebel Table. Even though the Brother was so close, we still managed to play up. We would squirt water, flick bread, peas or whatever and one night he caught me flicking peas across the table and once again called, "Bourke, front and center." Out I go.

The Brother was a little fellow with glasses. I was always tall for my age, so here I was, eye balling him and after he really dressed me down, he said in a much quieter voice, "Now, you get back to the table and if I catch you chucking food about again,

I'll kick you up the arse. Now get!"

I couldn't believe it and I was telling my mates he swore at me and I would repeat what he said.

When the meal was over, the boys would clear the tables, take everything into the kitchen, scrape and clean the plates and then wash and dry up. There was always a team to do it and anyone else who was on punishment. I liked it because it was something to do and I was used to it as we kids did it at home for Mum. After tea and cleaning up, you would go to the school room and do homework and study. They would close the room around 7.30 pm and you would have to get ready for bed.

When it came near to 8 pm the Brother would look at his watch, clap his hands loud and say, "Right boys." Everyone would have to go to the toilets, clean their teeth, then come back to their bed. When everyone was back and he was ready, I used to watch him every night, he would clap his hands for the second time and right on 8 pm everyone would say a quick prayer and get into bed. He would do another walk around and see that everyone was in bed, walk to the door and say, "Goodnight boys."

Everyone would reply, "Goodnight, sir." And look out for anyone found talking after lights out.

Where I slept I could look through the window across the courtyard and through another room. I could see the Brothers talking and smoking and that really got me. I used to say to my mate Ray next to me, "Hey, look at them drinking and smoking."

He got the wind up and wouldn't look. He would tell me to lie down and go to sleep.

I would have been there around six weeks or more and I got it in my head to take off. I had seen a couple of others who had taken off and got caught, but I never got around to talking to them. They were different boys when they bought them back. My mate, Ray, wasn't happy either and when I told him I was going to go he tried to talk me out of it.

It was early in the week and I was ready. I was going to take off after the Brother did his final check that was around 8.30 – 9 pm and then went to bed. They would always come in very quiet and walk around. If a bed was empty they would go straight to the toilets and hurry you up back to bed. So I was going to go some time after that. I never had a watch and couldn't see the big clock and it so happened it was later than I thought, otherwise I would have had second thoughts.

I got out of bed, shook Ray and asked him if he was coming and he said no. He wished me luck and off I went. It was pretty dark and real cold. I started trotting along the road and was glad when I got to the shop at the corner. A few dogs started barking and that put the wind up me.

I started down the mountain. It was a lot of bends and winding turns, sharp ones too. I had gone a long way I thought but it started to break day. I was travelling well not worried about anything and then I heard this car coming from behind me. I stopped and looked back and my heart missed a beat. I had an awful feeling in my gut because it was the Head Brother's green car. He had two seniors standing on the running boards, one either side of the car. One was the best fighter and the other the best runner. I knew I could outrun them because they couldn't catch me on the football field. I thought about taking off but to where? All I could see was steep and rocky slopes so I just stood and waited for him to stop right beside me.

"Good morning, Patrick."

"Good morning, Brother."

"Where are you going?" He asked.

"Home, sir."

"Well, get in," he says, "I'll take you back and you can get the bus."

So I got in and no one spoke all the way back. I was surprised how far I had gone and how far it was. We pulled up inside the garage and one of his bum boys locked the door. He dismissed them and said to me, "You go to my room and sit and wait for me."

Off he went and when he came to me I had had enough time to think of the trouble I was in and was even thinking of taking off again. While I was sitting there, I couldn't help but notice all the half empty bottles of grog and the full ashtrays. But you never ever saw any of the Brothers smoke through the day. I can't think of the Head Brother's name, but he was nice to talk to.

He comes in and the first thing he did was pick up this strap and started to strap his other hand. And then he sat down and started to ask me why I had done what I had. When I told him that I was homesick and didn't like the school and everything else, he just sat and looked at me. Must have been weighing up what I had said.

Then he said, "Righto. Stand up." And when I did I suppose he could see the fear in me.

He started strapping his hand again and said, "Do you know what we do with boys that run away from school?

I said no and he said, "I usually strap them but you, I won't."

God, I felt relieved because I had had the strap in class and boy could they use it. I had also seen other boys get it too.

"Instead, you will have no breakfast, you will get extra duties and you will also have a cold shower. Understood?"

I said, ""Yes, sir."

"Right, you go and report to Brother 'whoever' and he will take you from there."

Boy, was I glad to get out of his room. I went to who I was told to and he was very stern but real friendly. He took me to the dormitory and told me to get my towel and soap and to follow him. While we were going to the showers all the boys were playing and waiting to go to class. The word was out about me and boy, did they give it to me. Like:

"What happened, Bourke?"

"Did shanks pony go lame?"

"Did you get lost and come back?"

And of course: "You'll be sorry." Plus a lot more quips.

The Brother took me to the showers and said, "Right, get undressed." And I did and it was very cold – there was frost on the grass.

"Turn the tap on and get under."

That I did and he was standing there watching. He sings out to put plenty on and wash my hair. When I was finished he took me back to the dorm and said, "Now you can sweep it on your own and do it properly."

It used to always take two boys and sometimes they would put three on to sweep it. So I did it and did it properly the first time because we would have to get one of the Brothers to check and if they found they could see a little bit of dirt, all they would say is, "It's not done properly, do it again."

What they would do was get the sun behind them and stand back and being a polished floor, you could see where you missed. And I knew this, so that's what I did. When he cleared me he told me to go straight to class and boy, was I hungry come dinner time. I got heaps all that day but the Brothers didn't hold it against me.

But come the weekend they stopped me from playing football and that hurt and put the hate back into me. I told Ray that I was going to go again and next time they wouldn't catch me and that they never would.

It would have been a month or so after I had first bolted that I decided to go again. I was all geared up all day, never said a word to anyone. Come tea time I made sure I had a good meal and when it came time for bed, I told Ray. He hated the place as much as me but never had the guts to go. His mother was a barmaid in the Centurion Hotel in George Street, nearer to Adelaide Street, and that's where Pop used to drink on Friday and Saturday nights.

We went to bed and it was after the final check, around 9 pm. It was so obvious to me that the Brother always showed up at my bed, so this night he did the same but I pretended to be asleep. I watched for their lights to go out, gave them half an hour and I was ready and determined not to get caught again. I got out of bed, woke my mate and he said, "Good luck. I hope you do it this time."

It would have been 10 pm or after when I took off. I had my plan and I trotted all the way to the shop and I remembered the road from when they took us on a trip. It was very winding and a lot of sharp bends in it so when I came to the turns I started to go straight down, through and under a lot of boulders and rocks. I never fell once but I did do a lot of bum sliding. I did a lot of running and trotting and I was a long way along the road going flat out when daylight came. That's when I started to panic. Every time I heard a car coming from behind I would get off the road. If there were no trees to hide behind, I would lay on the ground until the car had passed. I was mainly looking for the green car as that was the only car that they had at the school. I just wasn't game to thumb a ride. In my school days there weren't many cars around and there weren't a lot of people living at the Mountain.

It was late in the morning when I got to Beenleigh. I walked through the outskirts and I didn't realise until it was too late but I was walking past the police station on the opposite side of the road. It was an awful feeling for me but it only made me walk all the faster. I saw the road sign saying Brisbane. I forget how many miles but I thought if I kept going I would be home late.

Walking along the road I kept on thinking of the police so I took note of a street name, picked a number and thought I would be Paddy Smith. It seem a long way but just when I could see the bridge I heard this motorbike coming so I jumped behind a big signboard and watched the bike go past with a sidecar on it. The man riding it had a khaki uniform on and I thought, he's right, he's a soldier, as there was still a lot of army fellows around. So I kept on walking straight across the bridge and on the Brisbane side was the toll house. The toll keeper was talking to the soldier on the motorbike.

They said, "Good day."

I replied and said, "I don't have to pay do I?"

He said no and then the soldier said, "Hey, come here son."

I walked across to him and when I got close to him I looked at his shirt collar and my heart went racing. I saw the number badge on his shirt. He must have known what was going through my mind because he said, "Come here, son, don't you run away."

So I went up to him and he said, "Where are you going?"

"Home, sir."

"Where's that?"

"Brisbane, sir."

"Where have you been?"

"To see my aunty."

"Where does she live?"

I told him the number and street name and her name was Maggie Smith, and that's when he said to me, "You come from the Brothers College don't you?"

I knew he had me because I had the school clothes on and it stood out a mile.

So he says, "Here, jump in and I'll take you back and you can go home by the train."

I was real happy with that idea so I jumped in the sidecar, something that I was used to doing. He took me straight to the police station, took all my particulars and told me to wait in the outer office.

I heard the sergeant ask the switch girl for the school and then the one-sided conversation I'll never forget.

"Hello Brothers. Sergeant ? of Beenleigh Police. I have one of your young fellows here, name of Paddy Bourke."

All I could hear was, "Oh yeah, oh yeah," three or four times and then again, "Eh, uh, ok and you don't want him back. So you will send his clothes home to him? Thank you."

By the time he came out to me and, as tired as I was and felt, I was very happy. He looked at me and said, "You heard did you?"

I said, "Yes, sir."

"You're happy are you?"

I said, "Yes, sir."

"Have you had anything to eat?"

I told him, "Not since tea last night."

So he took me over to the house and his wife made me a nice meal. I stayed in the house and played with his young daughter, 4 or 5 years old.

Around 2 pm in the afternoon the sergeant came and gave me a cold drink and said, "Righto Paddy, time to catch the train."

So his wife, who was very good to me, gave me a couple of lollies and said goodbye. The train was there and he put me in a compartment, gave me my train ticket and 6d and the last words he said were, "Now this train will take you to South Brisbane, that's as far as it goes. Don't you get off until then and one of your parents will be there for you. Goodbye and good luck."

So the train was off. All the way I could think of, if Pop was there waiting for me, what he would do to me. Every time the train stopped I would ask the oldie next to me, "Is South Brisbane next?" and she would say no.

She got sick of me asking her and said, "I will tell you when we come to the station before South Brisbane." So I just sat there thinking of what was in store for me from Pop.

Then the old lady said, "South Brisbane next stop."

So off I got and I walked over Victoria Bridge, down George Street and caught a tram at Roma Street. When I got off the tram at the Terminus, I saw Kathleen. She was getting the milk and bread and she said, "Didn't you see Mum?"

I said, "No, and where's Pop? Does he know?"

She said no and I felt happy then.

Poor old Mum comes home, does the usual and then says, "What are you going to do when your father finds out?"

I said I didn't know and she said, "Well, I know." I left it at that.

Pop came home around 6 pm and we were all having tea. When he walked in the kitchen and saw me sitting at the table all he said was, "What are you doing home?"

I said, "On school holidays, Pop," and that's all that was said.

About two weeks later I was in bed sound asleep and all of a sudden Pop had hold of my ear.

"You young bastard. I'll give you telling me bloody lies."

Did he get into me and was I yelling and screaming. Mum came in yelling and singing out, "Frank, Frank, leave him alone. You'll have the police down in a minute if you don't."

So he left me and went and lay down at the foot of his bed. He was just lying there puffing on a cigarette. I could see him from where I was sitting on the floor sobbing.

Pop says from the dark, "You little bastard, You tell me any more lies and I'll kill you."

I said in a sobbing voice, "I wish you hada killed me."

It only took him three or four steps and I heard him coming. He grabbed me by my throat and was shaking shit out of me. I was making all sorts of noises when once again poor old Mum was there stopping him. She told me to shut up and get into bed and that was the last hiding I ever got from my father. We all got our share but I think I was in front as the one who got the most.

Our Pop was never a vicious man but liked discipline and when he gave us a hiding you knew you had one. But I have always said, I never regret getting any of my hidings and that I never got as many as I deserved. And I learnt real early in my young days that the louder you screamed the better it made Pop feel.

That also brings me to my last days at school. I didn't go back after coming home from Mount Tambourine.

CHAPTER FOUR

Pop came home the day after giving me the big thrashing and said, "What are you going to do?"

I asked him if I could get a job – I was 13.

"You might as well, otherwise you'll have the police coming around again."

So I went and got myself a job on a dairy farm on the Brisbane River, close to Ipswich but I can't remember where it was. The farm belonged to a Mr Moran and his wife.

This is the start of my working career and my first ever job. Why I picked a dairy farm I will never know.

Mr Moran was a big man and his wife was a small woman and pregnant. That I knew because I had seen Mum and Mrs Briggs have quite a few babies. Mr Moran picked me up from the train station at Ipswich and we went out to his farm in a horse and cart. All dirt roads then except in the main street of town - that's all Ipswich was to me in those days. I think you could say that there was as many sulkies, drays and saddle horses around as there were cars.

We got out to the farm and his wife had the cows in and had started milking. Mr Moran showed me what he wanted and so we started. We milked 72 cows night and day. I forget how much milk we got but it was my job to do the separating. The separator that he had was a big one and he showed me how you had to turn the handle and to me it was hard and heavy but to see Mr Moran do it, it looked easy.

You had to turn the handle as fast as you could until the bell stopped ringing. When the bell stopped you turned the tap on from the big vat that we poured the milk in as you milked each and every cow. It would take me a good half hour or more to separate the cream from the milk. We would get nearly a full cream can every day. When I was doing the separating I had a big tin mug which I would half fill with fresh milk. Then while I was turning the handle I would hold the mug over the cream spout and fill the mug with fresh cream. I did that every day and never put on any extra weight. Mr Moran always said, "You'll get fat."

Mrs Moran stopped milking and stayed in the house as she got closer to having the baby so there was only Mr Moran and me.

Mr Moran used to sleep with no clothes on because it was so hot even then. They had a highset Queenslander and every night from around midnight on, he would come and wake me, then walk to the corner of the verandah. He would cup his hands around his mouth and sing out to the cows, "Come on, come on."

He would do that twice and by that time I would be up and lighting up the old wood stove. We would have our breakfast – he always liked his cup of tea. Then after cleaning up we both took the old hurricane lanterns which we would fill every night with kerosene. By the time we got to the gate at the dairy all the cows would be there waiting. Mr Moran would leg me up on to the big gate post and I would count the cows. If there were any missing he would say, "Go get the dogs." So I would and then we both would hunt the cows up to the yards.

The morning milking would start by the time we got the first six cows in the old bales and got everything ready. It would always be around the 1 am mark and we would be milking the first cow and all of a sudden you would hear a cow bellowing up the paddock and the dogs barking. And the next thing the cow, or cows, that were missing at the count would come in flat with their tails up over their backs so as the dogs couldn't swing off them. After that they would all come in every morning. I used to milk one for one with Mr Moran and he was real pleased with that as he said every other boy he had couldn't keep up with him.

Everything he did on the farm was done by horses. He ploughed, raked, cut, and loaded on to a big horse drawn trailer by pitch fork.

It was my job to take the cream cans up to a little shed at the main gate where the mail truck would pick it up and take it to the factory. I would put the cans on to a horse drawn sled and walk behind the horse. When I got to the shed I would pull the lid off the last can and then I would stick my fingers in the cream and have a good feed of fresh cream. I should have put on a lot of weight but never did. I was always around the seven stone mark and about 5' 3" and stayed like that for year.

When we finished the milking it was my job to separate, put the cream away in the old dairy, clean all the gear and then all the bales and yards. Mr Moran would go down the paddock and do the ploughing by horse – hard work it was. When I was finished I would go to the house and Mrs Moran would make me a good breakfast.

On my way down to the house I would take the cows down and put them in the paddock for the day. I would have a sleep after breakfast and Mrs Moran would wake me around 10 am and I would take smoko down to Mr Moran. He would come up to the house and have a sleep and around 1 pm we would start the day milking. That went on day after day and it sure made me tired. Sometime down the track Mrs Moran had the baby and he was real glad when she came home from hospital as he was doing the cooking and everything else around the place. She never came up to the milking for a good month but on her first morning she came up pushing the pram. She put the pram where she could keep an eye on the baby and started milking and boy, could she milk. After a while Mr Moran would leave us early and go and do his farm work. It made it easy on all of us.

I remember my brother, Frank, coming up one weekend and we were mucking around. Franky fell over and sprained his wrist. Mr Moran came and went crook and had to take Franky to the train. He wasn't impressed and said so.

I had my 14th birthday on the farm and Mrs Moran made me a nice cake. It wasn't long after that I left and I was glad but sorry; it was long hours but the work didn't bother me.

Just before I left, in the same week it was, Mr Moran got a new green tractor - a 16 disc plough. I didn't see it arrive. I took his morning tea down as usual and there it was. He was working it and he had started ploughing a fresh paddock and had finished about five or six rows when I turned up. He called me over to the machine and said, "Ever driven one of these before?"

I said no, so he said, "See this pedal, the clutch and the brake?"

And he gave me a run down on how it went then told me to get on her. I felt really good and he showed me what he wanted me to do.

He said, "Follow the furrow and if you can see me with my hands up like this, push both pedals in and hold them and the tractor will stop. Now off you go."

He sat under a big gum tree having his smoko. I had gone around twice and all of a sudden there he was with his arms up. So I did what he said and stopped.

He came over and said, "How you going?"

"Real good." I says.

"Missing anything?" So I look around and says no.

"How many discs you got?" I counted 15, one missing. He didn't get mad, all he said was, "Come on, we'll look for it."

We found all the missing parts, put it together and off he went. That was my first experience on a tractor.

I left that weekend and they both said that they were sorry to see me go. That was my first real job. When I got home Mum was glad to see me. Pop came home and was surprised to see me.

All he said was, "What are you going to do now?"

I said I would get a job around town. That I did as a messenger boy – pushing a pushbike around the town delivering and picking up parcels. I did that for a short time and gave it away. Then I saw an ad in the paper for someone looking for a cowboy – must be able to ride a horse and milk. Apply Australian Estates, Creek Street, Brisbane.

So I went home and asked Mum and she said, like always, "Go ask your father."

Pop was lying on his bed at the foot of the bed under the light. I was a bit windy of him as I didn't think he had forgiven me for running away from the College. "Pop, can I get a job out bush?"

He put his paper down and looked at me, like he did when he was serious. "Whereabouts out bush?"

I said I didn't know and that I had seen the ad. He thought for a minute and said, "I don't care, go ask your mother."

"She said to ask you." I said.

That's when he looked at me and said, "I suppose so but behave yourself and don't go getting into any bloody trouble." I was real happy when Mum said yes.

The next day I went into Australian Estates and after answering all the questions and getting a note of approval from Mum, they said I had the job. They gave me my train ticket and a lot of vouchers – three for each day on the train, one for each meal.

They gave me all the directions and instructions and told me if I stayed there three months my fare was paid for and another three months they paid my return fare. I was told I would catch the train at Roma Street Station, leave it at Rockhampton, catch another to Townsville, leave it and catch another train to Cloncurry, and get off there. I would stay the night at a hotel and catch another train to Selwyn, wait there and catch a mail truck to Chatsworth Station and a Mr Grimshaw would come and pick me up and take me to his station.

The day came when I was to go. I had a feeling in my gut, all geared up. Mum packed my port and strapped two army blankets to it. She gave me a few shillings, all she could afford, and took me into Roma Street in her sulky with the old gray mare, Flossy. She drove me right to the entrance and tied Flossy up to a tree. When we went into the train who should we meet but Teddy Lisk from the dairy. He had left the dairy working for his father, Bill, and got a job on the railway and stayed until he died a long time after. He was always full of jokes and fooling around. He gave me heaps, took me, Mum and Jimmy to my carriage. It wasn't until the train started to pull away and I saw my mum standing there waving and crying her eyes out that I realised what I was doing and wondered what I was in for.

The old steam train was packed. It had two long bench seats and a corridor that ran the full length of the carriage at the ends of which was the toilets. They had a dining car in the middle of the train. I can remember the first night. We left at 7 pm and when we had settled everyone was asking names and how far they were going and shaking hands. When it got around to me and I said that I was going to Cloncurry, they were all saying, my hadn't you got a long trip ahead of you and I still didn't realise how far I was going.

We got to Rocky at 11 am the next day. I got off the train and I had to wait until 4 pm that day to catch my next train to Townsville. That I did and I was in the same carriage as some of the people from the night before. I felt a lot better with the people I knew. I was very tired and buggered and I never got much sleep from the train ride. Very rough.

We got into Townsville the next day and I said goodbye to the people I got to know and they continued on to Cairns. There was a couple I still knew who got on the train for Cloncurry but they got off at Hughenden. I was on my own again and started to miss home. The train stopped at a siding and two old fellows got on. Real bushy little fellows they were. I think they could see I was upset and they started talking to me. One asked where I was going and what I was going to do and when I told him all about everything, he started to fire up his pipe and did it stink. He started telling me a story of his own.

"When I was a boy of your age I went out bush to work for this cocky and he told me if I stayed working for him for 12 months at 1/- a week, he would shout me a trip around the world. I stayed with him for two years and he gave me bugger all. So if you get out there and he doesn't want to pay you, you go to the nearest police station and tell them and they will get your money for you."

By the time they got off at Julia Creek they really had the jimmy shits up me and I started to have second thoughts about going out to the station. I was glad to see the pair go!

When the train got to Cloncurry it was very late in the afternoon. I can remember going up to the Station Master and asking him how much it was for a junior to Brisbane. He said it was £1-10. I counted my money and found I only had a few bob over a pound. So I wouldn't have anything to eat even if I did have enough for a train ticket. So I knew that I would have to carry on.

I don't know what the name of the hotel was that I stayed at but I will never forget my stay there. I booked into the hotel over the road from the railway as I had to catch my last train early in the morning around 6 am. The Station Master told me to ask the lady if she would she wake me early and she said she would. I had tea and went upstairs to my bed. What a night. I was that tired from the train trip I thought I would have fallen asleep straight away. But as soon as I got under the sheet and lay down I felt something biting me, like a sharp nip and in more than one place. I quickly got out of bed and turned the light on, pulled the sheets down and had a good look. I couldn't see a thing and got back into bed and after a short spell it happened again. I repeated getting in and out of bed four or five times and on the last effort I stood by the light switch, waited for a short spell and turned the light back on. When I did, on top of the bottom sheet was bugs, bed bugs they were. So I got my pillow and my two blankets and laid down on the verandah outside and went to sleep. I didn't sleep real well and was awake and waiting when the boss man came to wake me. Had my breakfast and went over to the railway station. The train was waiting for the mail to come and wouldn't be long they told me.

So once again I was off and I was on my own all the way. I was on a goods train and it stopped at every spot along the way. We got to Selwyn after midday and I had to wait at the station until the mail trucks came. There were two Internationals KB Models – 8 tonners. But I would say they had a lot more than that on. There were two brothers, Alf and Bert Weld, and they were off to Boulia Town. I gave them a hand to load and they tarped up and off we went. We were well along the road and it started to rain. The further we went the heavier it got. Next thing I know, they are racing alongside each other, side by side. We were on a claypan, water everywhere. It was real fun. They were making a lot of hand signs to each other and they were pushing the trucks as fast as they could go.

Next thing I know we were doing a full 360 turn. I never thought two fellows could have so much fun. Then all of a sudden the strong winds hit them and ripped the tarp off Alf's load. We pulled up and they tied it down again and they said that they better move fast as the rain started to really belt down harder.

We got to Chatsworth Station late in the afternoon. I always remember when we pulled up at the storeroom and the bookkeeper was waiting. He said he had never seen so much rain. He raced out to the rain gauge and it was full to the top but I don't know how much they got. They gave me a feed and also a bed and said I would have to wait for the road to dry out before Mr Grimshaw could come and get me. And that he did late the next day. He had a big black Buick Straight 8 - beautiful car to ride in. We got to his house late, had tea and he took me down to my hut a good walk from the homestead. I was on my own and in the dark.

I was that tired from the trip and I thought I would have no trouble going to sleep. But when I lay down I could still feel the motion of the train still bouncing along!

I got on real well with the Grimshaws but after a week he told me that I was not what he wanted. He said that they should not have sent me and that he was writing to the Australian Estates to complain. He wanted an experienced man, one that could muster and work and repair the machinery and that he was going to start mustering for his shearing in another two weeks. He was more worried that he would spend more time looking for me lost in the paddocks than he would looking for sheep and that his place had good sized paddocks. He wasn't sending me home but taking me back to Chatsworth as they wanted a cowboy.

When I arrived at Chatsworth they took me to this old hut a long way from the main house with corrugated iron roof and walls. I walked around the station all day and late in the afternoon while I was walking around I met my first real black fellow. I told him where I was camping and he says, "You come down to our camp, mate, and we look after you. Come down after tea." And he showed me where his campsite was. I didn't know it at the time but it turns out that I was talking to King Moonlight. He was king of the Bourke Tribe and his wife's name was Narda. They had kids everywhere.

That night after tea I went to my bed and as I was lying there in the pitch dark, it started to get windy, blowing real hard. Every time a gust of wind blew, the whole side of the building would move backwards and then would fall back with a loud bang. I got a bit frightened so decided to go to the black fellows' camp. So I lit my hurricane kerosene lamp and away I go. As I was walking I thought I could see a light and I would stop and look and go again. I did this quite a few times. It was definitely a light but every time when I stopped, it stopped. Being in the dark I couldn't see properly and I panicked, started singing out real loud. All of a sudden there were people all around me from the homestead. So after they settled me down, the boss said to get my gear and take me down to the head stock man's quarters. And that's where I met Mr Walker, the head stock man of Chatsworth. He was a nice old fellow, very tall and real thin. Every time I saw him he had a cigarette in his mouth.

The bookkeeper was in the same hut and he was doing the milking. He said he'd show me what to do in the morning. So, early next morning he gets the milk buckets, takes me to the stockyard run with all these cows in and starts to milk them.

He said, "I'll milk the first few and then show you."

He didn't ask me if I could milk so I just watched him. Then he said, "Come here, Paddy, and I'll show you how to strip them."

I wasn't silly so I thought I'd let him milk as they had 13 cows. They never gave much milk and they weren't good cows in the bales. They would all shit and kick and flick the tail – everything a good milker doesn't do. So every morning for the first week he would come up to the main milking and watch me try to strip the last few and I was doing an awful job of it. Then one morning I was up, had the cows in and was waiting for him to come. He was running late so I thought I would start – give him a surprise. I was milking away and looking around the back of the cow the way he would come, I was really into it, when I looked around behind me and there he was, looking through the rails at me.

All he said was, "You cunning little bugger." And walked off. That was the joke for a long time.

One morning I was on my way to the cows and up past the machinery shed and the saddle shed there was all these swags everywhere. Fellows would stick their heads out and say, "Good day mate. Where you going?"

They were all black fellows. Turned out the mustering camp was in and there were 16 men and that's when I first met the only jackaroo on the place.

I got to know a lot of the blacks and I also used to play with Narda's boys after I did all my chores as I could do what I liked. One morning while we were playing this young fellow came racing into where Narda was working in the laundry. Narda was ironing and she had the copper boiling with clothes in it. And he starts singing out, "My tail, my tail!"

Narda bent down to the fire and pulled out this black looking stick and gave it to him. He took it outside and started to cut it into pieces. He gave me a bit and that was my first bit of kangaroo tail.

One morning while I was pulling my boots on I was sitting on the top step of the hut. You could see Moonlight's camp – it was among the gums on the river in front of the station. I could see old Narda leaving the camp and next thing she's running to the dogs, lets one go and she starts to sool him onto a big roo. The poor dog started racing around, cocking his leg on every tree. He came near and Narda was singing out to him. With all the noise she was making and all the other dogs barking, the roo took off. Narda started rousing on the dog. "You bloody mongrel. All you want to do is piss, piss all the bloody time."

She got hold of him, gave him a hiding and put him back on the chain. It sounded funny being early in the morning and the way she spoke.

Another day one of the oldies stopped me and said in his broken English, "Hey, mate. You go to the shop and get me plug of sunshine tobaccy." And he gave me a shilling. I did what he wanted and got this small plug of black, hard tobacco and 3d change. I gave it to him and watched him cut a bit off and start chewing it. It was pay day and he had his money, all two bob pieces locked together with a big rubber band so they weren't overpaid.

When smoko or dinner time came all the whites would go inside and sit down away from all the flies, and there were millions of them. You would stop at the screen door, grab a towel that was there all the time and for that one purpose, and bash your back with it, then quickly duck inside. Meanwhile, all the blacks would stand around and wait for the cook to hand them their tucker then they would go and sit around anywhere outside and eat it.

Another time when the camp was in, they were getting everything ready to go back out mustering. They had men everywhere doing something like shoeing horses, repairing pack saddles, packing the pack saddles with stores. I was standing at the tie rail outside the saddle shed and Mr Walker was there.

I must have driven him mad with all the questions like, "Good day Mr Walker. What are you doing?"

"You got eyes, boy."

"Yes, Mr Walker. What are those things?"

"Pack saddles, boy."

"What do you do with them?"

Paddy Bourke

He told me and then I asked him, "How many horses you got, Mr Walker?"

"You go to school, boy?"

"Yes, Sir."

"Didn't they teach you how to count?"

"Yes, Sir."

"Then you go and bloody well count them and then come and tell me."

So with that answer and the way he gave it, I shut up. Next thing he did something I will never forget. He was busy coming and going in and out of the shed and I was still standing near the door of the saddle shed. Mr Walker came out and told this big bugger, "Jacky, you catch this horse and do whatever."

This Jacky was a lot taller and heavier man and younger than Mr Walker. He was busy working on another horse he had tied up and as he kept walking away from Mr Walker he mumbled something that Mr Walker heard but I didn't. All Mr Walker did was walk into the shed, was in there for a short time, come out, walked straight up to the big fellow and said, "Jacky."

When the big fellow turned to face him he started belting the shit out of him. He had a side line chain strapped to his wrist. Jacky grabbed it and next thing Mr Walker into him with his other arm that also had a chain strapped to it. The commotion and noise that they made stopped all the other fellows and not a one went near them. Mr Walker flogged the piss out of Jacky and it frightened me so I took off running to the house and kept out of their way.

That night while Mr Walker and the bookkeeper were sitting on the steps having a smoke and talking, I was sitting down from them and I said to Mr Walker, "That was a cruel thing you did to that man."

He explained to me in a nice but stern way, "You wouldn't understand, boy. I gave him an order and he told me no. If I had let him get away with that, I might as well not go out again. There's 18 men in the camp and there is only one other white, he's a jackaroo and wouldn't know much more than you. So the next time I tell any one of them to do something they will." And he was right.

I had been at Chatsworth nearly three months or more. I used to write home to Mum and looked forward to getting her letters. Then I started to get homesick and the longer I stayed the worse I got. So I told the boss I wanted to go home and he said, "Righto. Will put you on the next mail." That was a week away and boy, a lot happened in that week.

It was very dry and they were pumping water for the cattle and also carting water for the homestead. Berty Web got a job on the station. He was a real nice and funny bloke. He would take me with him on the truck whenever I finished my chores.

This day we were heading out to a mill some 30 miles out. He had a big tank on the back. As we were going along I looked to the back and saw the tank moving to one side and told Berty. He said, "Here, move over."

I said, "I can't drive."

"Just sit here and steer it."

He told me what to do and, just like Mr Moran did on the farm with the tractor, gave me my first drive of a truck. I stayed there for quite a while until we came to a river crossing and Berty took over.

The next day we had to cart water for the main house so we put the big water tank on the back of the truck and off we went. Five miles or more down the road we came to the bore and it had a big tank full. Berty got on the low side and he syphoned it into the tank on the truck. We had King Moonlight with us. He was a nice old fellow, had no teeth at all and would suck his lips – it looked quite funny. We finished filling the tank and Berty and I got in and had a good swim. The weather was real hot and steamy. When we got back to the house Berty had to use a big hose to suck the water from the truck to the house tank. He was sucking like hell and better than the windmill. Old Moonlight and me were laughing and going on at the antics and expressions of Berty so he said, "Here, you have a go." And he gave the hose to me.

Then the joke was on me. I tried for a while but did no good. Berty said, "Come on Moonlight, you have a go." Well, he did and to see him trying to suck and see the expressions on his face. He was sucking and blowing and making all sorts of noises. Berty and I couldn't stop laughing and it was very funny.

Next thing old Moonlight got very angry and savage. The look changed and he started gibbering. Berty couldn't understand him. All of a sudden, Berty bent down, grabbed the pick by the head and gave it a bang on the floor. The pick fell to the floor and it left Berty with the pick handle in his hand. Then he held it in both hands and even I knew what it meant. Moonlight quickly shut up. He looked at Berty then me, then the pick handle and as quick as you like, he jumped off the truck and I never ever saw him again.

I asked Berty, "Would you have used that?"

"Bloody oath! And he knew it too. He's a bad old bugger when he starts."

The end of the week couldn't come quick enough for me. They all said goodbye and I was off on my way home. Because I stayed well over three months, they paid my fare and all I had to do was pay for my tucker.

CHAPTER FIVE

When I got home Mum and all the younger ones made me feel welcomed. I had a spell for a week or two and decided I would have another go at bush life. So I went to Australian Estates again and this time they sent me out to Goondiwindi to a place called Mt Carmel owned by Ron Fee. I am not sure but it could be McFee.

It was a returned soldier's block for any returned servicemen. They used to ballot for them and Ron drew his. It was about 40 miles from Goondiwindi, was 5540 acres of Brigalow, Belah and some Gidgee timber. A very good block and Ron had 5,000 big wether sheep and a few milkers. I was sent out there as a cowboy.

Ron came to town and picked me up from the train station. He was only young and had been a pilot through the war. He did what they all do when they first meet you, asked me about my previous work what schooling I had. We were on his block when he asked me how many blankets I had. I said I had two.

"Oh good, we better pull up at the woolshed and get you a couple of wool packs as it gets pretty cold here."

We got to the woolshed but all it was, was an old cowshed with a couple of shearing stands, a wool press and an old set of sheep yards and catching pens. We were walking towards the shed and he said, "I better light a match. We don't want to step on an adder."

My ears priced and I said, "What did you say?"

He said, "I don't want to walk on a death adder."

Straight away in a very few quick steps, I was back in the ute. He came back to me and asked what was wrong. I told him the story I heard Mrs Briggs telling my Mum. Her Uncle Arthur Briggs was riding his motorbike along a gush road and an adder sprung up and bit him on the back and he died straight away.

Ron laughed his heart out and said, "Rubbish. You stay here and I'll get your packs and then I'll show you what an adder can and will do."

When we got to the homestead I met his wife, a lovely lady in every way. The only man he had was a Bill Watson from town and he was really good to me. Ron told them my story and they all started laughing. So at least I had made somebody happy!

The very next day while we were driving out, they spotted an adder on the road and Ron said, "We'll show you your first adder."

They both picked up a stick and then started playing with the adder. He was a foot or more long, dark in colour and thick. They stirred him up and then they would put the stick near his body and try and get it away before he could strike it. And he was nearly always too quick for them. When they had their fun with him he was buggered. Ron gave me a bit of platted fence wire, about a foot long and said, "Come and kill your first adder." And that I did.

He saw that I could ride a horse all right so he and Bill would show me how to find my way around the bush; showing me how to read the sun; what to do if I lost my horse; what to do if I got turned around while mustering. And never go through a fence unless I really knew where and which way I was going.

Within the first week that I was there he gave me this big horse called Raven to ride. He was a tall one and I found it easier to get on him from tree stumps or logs and water troughs. He got used to me doing it and would always get and stay close for me.

Ron and Bill were erecting windmills, 40 footers. They were putting two up at a time, setting the legs up in cement, then going on to the next one until they got the frames started. Then they would stay on the one until they had it finished. While they were doing that I was mustering the sheep on to the waters with the troughs on them. That's where he had the holding pens. He and Bill would come to me and we would go through the mob looking for all the fly struck sheep. He showed me how to use the dagging shears, clean the strike part, dress it and let it go. So I learned a lot about fly strike

I learned something new every day while I was there and they treated me very well. Bill and I lived in an old garage on a dirt floor. The station had no power, only kerosene. Everything ran on kero. We both had a lantern each and once it got dark we went nowhere without it.

Every night about 7 pm Ron would cooee out, "Tea time." Both Bill and I would grab our lanterns and snake killers, which was the platted wire five foot long. They had them hanging up everywhere around the homestead and all the time that I was there if we didn't kill an adder going, we would kill one coming back from tea. I never knew a place to have so many adders and I soon learnt that it's a lot easier to kill an adder than it was to kill a brown snake.

Mrs McFee used to kill them in the garden and around the house. Every time she did, she would hang them on the clothesline so that Ron would see them when he and Bill came home and he would make a fuss about it.

I don't think they were long married and they hadn't been there long because everything was new, the house, the tanks and stand. The garden was just starting to grow. Mrs McFee looked after everything in the house, yard and my jobs were the dogs, chooks, firewood and anything that Mrs McFee needed. I would milk one cow and she would milk four gallons, or near to it and between the two of us we would fill the milk buckets and four gallon tin. I would strain what milk the house needed and the rest we put on the arga stove. Mrs McFee would do the rest. When it was ready she put it to one side with a cloth over it and when it was cold, we would skim all the cream from the top. The milk that was left was fed to the dogs and chooks. That was something else I learnt and it was a lot easier than separating.

As soon as I finished all my chores I would catch my horse, grab a dog and would go and meet Ron and Bill and be out working in the paddocks all day.

We were having breakfast one morning and Ron said, 'Quick, Paddy, come with me." He took off in the ute and that's when he told me that his neighbour had been bitten on the foot by an adder. So I opened all the gates and left them open. We got to the house and the neighbour was just sitting there waiting for us with a tourniquet on his leg. His wife was away and he was on his own. Just got down at the table to eat breakfast and the adder hit him. We raced back and I closed all the gates. Ron dropped me off and he continued on towards town. He met the ambulance along the way and they took him into town. He was back out working in three days with no ill effects. I am not sure but I think his name was Harold Hungerford.

Ron did his shearing at his other neighbour's shearing shed and it worked out real good. I think his name was Doug McTaggart but I can't recall the name of his property. Wyaga was one of the big names around that area. I know that when he sold his wool he got a good price. That's when the wool prices were worth a £ a pound and all the cockys were making a fortune.

After we finished shearing there wasn't much horse work and they started to work me around the house. I didn't like that much so I decided to leave. They didn't want me to go and when I did go I was sorry as I had got used to those two. I was with them for seven months when I headed back home and was real glad to see Mum and Pop again.

I had a holiday at home for a while and next thing I know, Pop had a job to go to at St George. I went to town and got a job from the Australian Estates again. It was at Goondiwindi again but about 35 miles west. I was glad as I went on the same train as Pop. I went to a place called Gidi Gidi Station owned by Edgar McIllveen. He was alright but the women were really up themselves, like a lot of them because just after the war there was plenty of work around and most of all, everyone had a quid.

The cockys were making plenty of money as the wool prices really jumped. The cockys bought big cars whether they needed them or not and took trips overseas. Mrs McIllveen senior was one of those 'snobs'. They would have parties and invite everyone around. I had to help prepare for a couple of them and then clean up after them.

One day, before one of these parties, she says to Edgar, her son, "I'll take Paddy for the day as I want him to clean the garden up at this time."

I was around 15 years and hadn't done a bit of gardening and I hold her this. Edgar was standing beside me when I said, "Mrs McIllveen, I don't know a plant from a weed and I have never done any gardening before."

I really think she thought I was trying to get out of it so she said in her haughty, taughty voice, "Oh, you'll be alright. You'll learn."

Edgar says, "Mum needs you, so you give her a hand."

It was my job as I was the cowboy and cowboys' jobs were always around the house and if they needed you, they would get you out in the paddocks. I was pretty good on a horse and could find my way around without getting lost. This is what they liked so instead of going mustering, I had to stay and do some gardening.

Mrs McIllveen was a very keen gardener and you could tell by the way she had it all set up. They had very nice green lawns, manicured, but nobody could or would sit around as this place was full of funnel webs, big redbacks and once again, adders and brown snakes. You could see the spiders everywhere.

"Anyway," she says. "I'll get you to clean this bed up for me."

I honestly didn't know a plant from a weed and told her so again.

"You'll be right. Come and tell me when you're finished that one bed."

So I put my head down, arse up and got into it. Anything that I could tell was a plant I left. Anything else I just pulled out. I was nearly finished that one bed and she came out to check on me. When she saw what I had done, didn't she bang on it.

"Oh my God, look what you've done! Look at all my precious plants." She started to name them off.

When she had finished berating me, all I said to her was, "Mrs McIllveen. I did try to tell you that I know nothing about gardening." And with that she told me to get and go and see Edgar.

I was no good to her so I didn't stay there long, only a month before I finished. She got Edgar to get me to go out and cut some firewood and Edgar said to me, "Go and do what you can and keep her happy." So I walked down the paddock with the axe and stone, cut a bit of wood then jammed the axe head into the log and broke the handle.

They had a couple of bad horses on the place and Edgar decided to get Johnny Roberts, who, at that time was Australia's leading buck jump rider, a red head. He was going to come up on the weekend and make a day of it. There were a lot of people from town and all around who turned up to see Johnny ride the outlaw of Gidi Gidi.

I ran the horses and Edgar and I drafted them off and had them all ready. Everybody was making a day of it and there was plenty of grog about. Johnny got there on dinner time (lunch) and after lunch he came out with his two brothers, Kenny and Arthur. Kenny had a good pick up horse, a chestnut, nice looking horse. I went with them and Johnny caught and saddled the big brown in the yard and led him out a good ways from the yards. We were in an open paddock and black soil.

As he was going through the part of checking his gear, you could see him shaking and he said to Kenny, "If this mongrel takes off, you get me off and be quick."

He was really keyed up so he blindfolded the horse. I held him while he got on. Kenny was on his horse waiting and when John had finished moving around in the saddle, he pulled his hat down, sat back, looked around and said, "Let 'em go."

As soon as the blindfold came off, the horse looked around and Johnny hit with his spurs - a good pair of goose neck. It was good to watch and it all happened in a couple of seconds. As soon as Johnny hit the horse with the spurs he did a flying root, started to buck and just as quick, took off bolting across the paddock. It took Kenny by surprise as he wasn't expecting the horse to take off so fast. All you could see was Johnny spurring like mad trying to make the horse buck but all he did was make him go faster.

Everyone could hear him yelling out, "Kenny, get me of this thing! Kenny, where the hell are you!"

Kenny was singing out to him, "I'm trying, I'm trying." It took him a while but he got Johnny off before they got to the timber.

While I was living at Gidi Gidi I got to know the family on the property next door. It was called *Emoh Ruo*, which is *Our Home* spelled backwards and they were a real bushy and wild family of girls and boys. I would go there on a Saturday and stay till Sunday. Mrs Littlewood was a real homely woman and reminded me a lot of Mum. There was a girl, Thailee, who was 13, and her grandfather who was 80 years old. One morning they stepped off 50 paces and their grandad could shoot an empty 303 shell off the top of a stump, standing upright. He would use a .22 rifle and Thailee would do it in reverse – she would shoot with a .303 rifle and knock a .22 shell of the tree stump. It was good to see.

I left the McIllveens' and was glad I ended up back in Goondiwindi. After they took my fares and everything out I had very little money left. I booked into a place called Bushells Boarding House, run by Mrs Bushells, another nice old lady. I thought I would get a job fairly quick but there wasn't much around for me, being so young. So, every day I would have to clean up and go down town and see all the agents and then sit around. I got to know this old pensioner – Ned was his name. I would sit and talk to him and go for walks until the afternoon, then around three o'clock go and see the agents again. They were all good to me and told me to keep coming back as something would turn up. I was there for three days, had very little to do and was getting very hungry.

One morning, about 10 am, Ned and I were sitting outside in the gutter of the Squatters Pub, which is still there today. Old Ned says, "It's hot here. Come on, we'll go to the back and get in the shade."

When we got around the back there was an old, low shed with a wooden floor and it had a lot of plants and greenery around and this is where Ned liked to be as he had his gear there

Ned was lying back on the bed and I was sitting on the floor some distance away. "It's pensioner day," he said.

"Oh, yeah," I said. It didn't mean a thing to me.

"Yeah, I got paid. Come over here."

I said, "No."

Then I looked over towards him and he had his shaft in his hand and then he said to me, "If you help me out, I will give you half of my pension."

With that I took off. He frightened the hell out of me. Every day after that I would steer clear of him. I often think of him and think what I would do now. I would help him out in more ways than he'd like and I'd take more than half his pension. But it was good for me as it taught me never to trust anybody.

On the fifth day I was getting desperate and thought if I could get over to St George I could stay with Pop and be able to look for a job. I had an old fellow ask me could I light a fire and boil the billy. I said I could so he said he would give me a job as a gofer in a ring barking camp. He had six men and himself. So I threw my gear on the back of the truck waiting for all the men to get on who were somewhere still in the pub. Then all hell broke loose. This big loud mouth came along yelling and shouting and telling the boss to get the men and get out to the property. He was really going off his brain. Then he looked at me and asked, "What's that bloody boy doing there."

He was told, "I am taking him out as a billy boy."

"If he can't use a bloody axe, get him off."

So the boss came up and said, "Sorry boy, but my boss says I can't take you."

So I got my gear off and that's when I learned it was the arrogant Bill Gunn, later Big Bill Gunn. None of the fellows had anything nice to say about him.

I had to go back to the boarding house as I was too frightened to stay in the town now because of that poofter, Ned, who was still sitting there.

I met a man up at the railway station – I was up there finding how much the fare was to Thallon – and he must have seen that I was upset and asked me what the problem was. I told him and also about Ned and he asked me if I had a port.

I said, "Yes.

He said, "Well, you meet me here tonight, when the train is here. I'll swap your port for mine and get your train ticket for you." He got in a cab and took off.

I had to go and tell Mrs Bushells that I couldn't pay her. I told her I couldn't get a job here and I wanted to get over to St George to my Pop. She started asking me questions and it turned out she knew Pop well – she had gone to school with him and knew all his family. So I did what I told her I would do – I went out the back and cut her wood pile up to small wood for her fire. She sat me down to my first real meal in five days and I can never forget her for that.

I was at the station early, well before train time. Then the train pulled in and there still wasn't any sight of the man who was going to give me my ticket. I was going to jump on if he didn't show. Right at the last minute he came running up to me and said, "Here's your ticket. Quick, jump in here."

As soon as we get in the train was on its way, he straight away said, "Get your gear out." And we changed ports over. He gave me something to eat and told me that when I get off the train at Thallon, to look for a bloke named Bobby Rodney. "Give him a hand to load his truck and he'll take you over to St George that afternoon." That's what I did and got to St George that afternoon and had a good meal with my Pop who was very surprised to see me

The next day Pop gave me a couple of bob and told me to go and see Norman Howe, the Chinese shopkeeper in the main shopping block. That I did and he told me to go and see Old Billy Lindores and that meeting started a new and very good chapter in my life.

The Lindores brothers were shearing contractors who had two shearing teams working and Old Bill ran one of the teams for his eldest son, Billy Jnr. I was put on as a roustabout and put on the board picking up and sweeping the board for four shearers and sometimes five. I loved it from the start. I was always very fast on my feet and had no trouble doing the job. I got on real well with Old Bill and the rest of the men.

They stuck to the same men all the time. Young Bill was the No. 1 team. He had all the top shearers. They were fast and didn't muck about much. Whereas Old Bill had a good team of steady shearers. Two or three of them were quite happy shearing their 120 a day.

I found the tucker unreal and the best you could get anywhere. We had a good cook, a big, happy fellow, Bill Stevens. He liked to play cards for money and was a good player but a bad looser. He got very cranky when things went bad on him. I was taught by him and all the other fellows in the shed. Bill Stevens could stack the cards but wasn't game and wouldn't do it with us.

He came to me in a bar of the Royal Hotel one night and said, "Quick, Snap," This was the nickname they gave me and it stuck to me all the time I was in St George.

"Come and sit in on this game of yuraka. We need someone to make a game of four."

He said, "All you got to do is sit there and I'll do the rest. This bloke's got a quid on him and I'll show him how to spend it."

I knew then what he was going to do and he did do it. That was another experience for me and one I didn't like. I told Bill so and never played with him again. He could and would stack the cards while you were looking at him.

I would go out and do a shed – they mainly took three to four weeks to finish. When we came to town I would always stay with Pop and his old mate and good friend of the Bourke family, Paddy O'Connor. Pop and Paddy had done a lot of gold mining here and in New Guinea too. They were sinking all the foundations for the big weir in the Bellone River. They lived in old army barracks set up on the banks of the river about a mile downstream and just back a bit from the old wooden bridge that always went under water when it rained – and it did a lot in those days. When they started there were six of them went out. Ted Laye, the boss, he was with the water board and a mate of Pop's. Also, there was Ted, Pop, Paddy, my two older brothers, Tommy and Jimmy, and Keith Capp. He lived with us for years and was one of the family.

The three boys never stayed there long, they didn't like the tucker or the living conditions. So that left Pop and Paddy to dig the holes. Some of them that I saw were down 80 feet. I don't know what they finished up doing.

I was there one day and Pop was down the hole, 80 foot, and Paddy was up top on the windlass. They were talking to each other and I heard Pop say he was having some trouble setting the dynamite. When Pop sang out that he was right, he got in the bucket and held on to the rope. Paddy started winding the windlass. It seemed to be going too slow for me so I said I'd give him a hand to pull him up. Paddy said, "He's right. You go and sit down over there." And next thing Pop was to the top of the hole.

That was the first time I saw Pop down a hole that deep. They casually walked over to where I was under a tree and sat there having a smoke. All of a sudden there were three loud bangs and we had to sit there a bit longer and then the last of them went off.

I was up town and although I was only around 16 at the time, I used to go drinking in the pubs – there were five of them. I used to always mainly drink in the Metro and that was the roughest pub in town. Always see a fight or two and on any day of the week.

It was my turn to shout and when I went for my money I found I had lost my roll. I didn't know how much I had lost but I knew it was a fair bit. I left and started walking home back over my tracks. Half way home along the river road I came across Pop. He was heading up town.

"Where you going?"

"Home," I said.

"Come up here with me."

As we were walking I kept on going through my pockets. When Pop said, "You got any money?"

I said, "No."

He asked if I had lost some. When I said yes, he said, "Here." And handed me my roll.

Then he gave me a lecture on how to look after my money. He told me to put it in the bank.

"You go to the Post Office and tell the Post Master I sent you. He'll look after you."

So the next day, Saturday, I did just that and put £75 into my first ever bank account with the Commonwealth Bank. I kept £10 for myself. That's how much I had lost and how much Pop gave me back.

He said later on that night, "I thought I found a bloody fortune." He always walked looking down, looking for gold we reckoned.

CHAPTER SIX

I was with the Lindores for nearly nine months. They were only paying me a boy's wage so I left and went onto another property, a place at Windy Golly half way between St George and Thallon. I was on Wellington's property, good people too. They treated me well and I was always out in the paddocks – that's what I liked doing.

I met a cast fellow there by the name of Billy Hudson and who I thought was his wife but turned out he was only living with her.

One day Billy said to me, "Paddy, you have a long way to go, so if you're working for this fellow here and the bloke over the fence offers you a shilling a week more, then you take it and if you're worth it your boss will match it or better it." That was something I always did in my working days.

I left there and went back to St George. I met up with a returned soldier name of Neville Winks, a top bloke. We went out to Thomby Station, a very rough and scrubby place. The name of the manager was Charlie Tiller who had been there for lots of years and a tough one to work for. There was a married couple there and when we met them the woman turned out to be Billy Hudson's wife, or so I had thought. But in the couple of weeks that I had in town, she had got back with her husband, a Hockey Dillon, a one-eyed half cast. He turned out to be a real bad bugger.

One night they were arguing and Hockey doused her in kerosene and she took off screaming towards Thomby Creek. The homestead was built on its banks. It had a pontoon and she was heading for it. He was drunk and he was abusing and yelling at her. She was screaming and running. There was old Podge McEwan and Neville and me and Podge said, "Bugger 'em. Keep out of it."

Hockey couldn't catch her which was just as well as he was lighting and throwing wax matches. They were hard to put out and were very good in wet conditions. In later years they were banned – too dangerous. She hit the pontoon flying, got to the end and didn't even look back. She jumped in, swam to the other side and stayed there till morning.

That was something to see and never forget. The next day they buddied up and carried on as if nothing had happened!

We were mustering and getting ready for shearing. It took some time to clean the paddocks and then Charlie tells us all one night that the place has been sold and the new owners would be coming up to have an inspection. That they did and on the Saturday morning Neville and I were heading to the yard and we passed Charlie and another fellow all dressed up in white moleskins, good boots and tie. It didn't take much to work out who he was – one of the new owners.

As we passed them Neville said in a clear voice, "Good morning." Both of them ignored us and kept on walking.

Neville stopped, looked back and said, "I'll be - ! I fought for arseholes like them and they can't even say good day."

He yelled out, "Hey, Charlie!"

They stopped and looked back at us and Neville said, "Come here."

Charlie came back on his own. Neville said, "Did you hear us say good morning?"

"Yes, but we were busy discussing things."

"Yeah, well if we are not good enough to say good day to, then you can shove your job and everything else up your arse. We're finished."

"Oh, God, don't do that, we need you. We are starting to shear on Monday. Hang on."

He walked to his mate and said something to him and they came back to us. He introduced both of us and said, "This is your new boss and owner, Les Griffith." Neville just looked at him and said, "I don't give a – who it is, we're both still going."

That was mail day and that's what we did. Turned out the Griffiths owned the Toowoomba Foundry and both father and son came up. I bet they never forgot their first day at Thomby. We had been out of there a couple of months and found out later they sacked Charlie, that's what kind of snobs and people they were.

Back in town and the following Saturday we were drinking in the Metro. We were drinking with a constable, a Darcy Nolke. He played with the All Whites A grade rugby league – played on the wing. He was a mate of Neville's.

Just after lunch he said, "I got to go on duty this arvo." He was half tanked then.

We carried on drinking and about three in the arvo, he and the sergeant were doing the rounds and they stopped outside the side door. The pub had a front door and a back door that led out to the back and you could end up on the street around the corner from where they stood looking in. I thought they were looking at me. I had a glass of beer to my lips and was pretty drunk. I still don't know what I did with the glass, whether I dropped it or handed it to someone. But the fear of the cops from my school days flashed back to me and I took off out the back out near Nipper Wilson's café. I stopped there because I had lost my hat and it was lying on the ground 20 paces or more back.

Next thing the sergeant came and picked up my hat and said, "Here, boy. Here's your hat." He just stood there holding it out to me.

I said, "No thanks, you can have it." And I started to trot off towards the river.

Next thing I heard this fellow yelling out to me to stop. I looked back and saw Darcy in his uniform. I really started to run flat out. Darcy was reaching out and just could not grab my shirt. I cut across the gutter at the Post Office and they had just done the road up and it had a lot of pea gravel. Only because I looked back, he would never had caught me but I slipped and fell. No sooner had I hit the ground when Darcy had me. He lifted me up and was shaking hell out of me. Between breaths, for he was

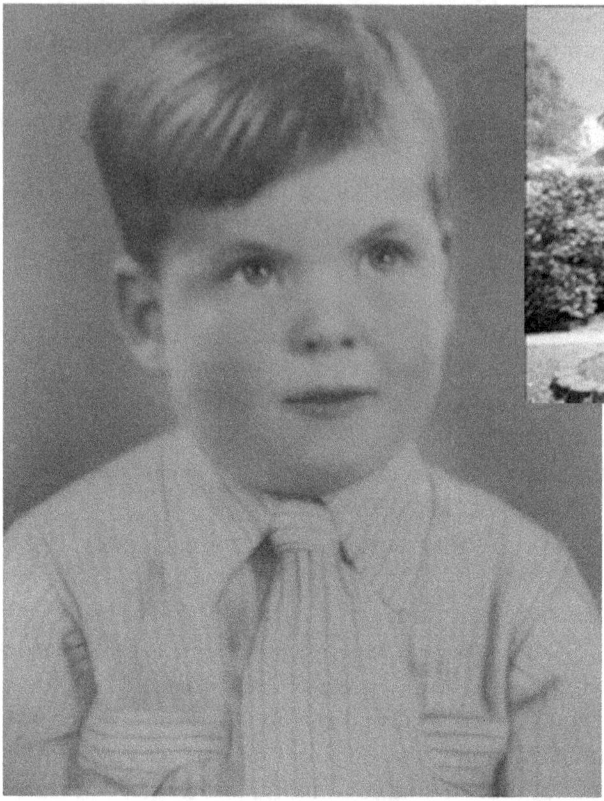

St Josephs School

Paddy at 4 years old

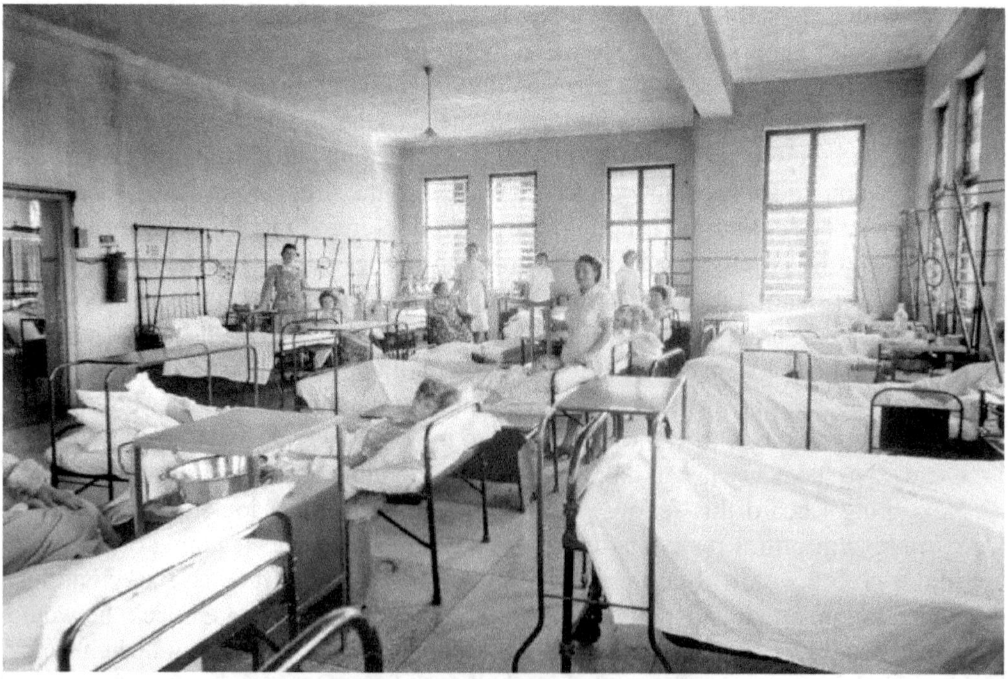

Brisbane General Hospital, 1946

Tram at Waterworks Road terminus, Ashgrove, Brisbane, 1929

Womblebank

Chatsworth in 1911

Paddy Bourke

Hotel Corones, Charleville

Clarendon, 1943

Paddy breaking in horses at Dililah

Nindigully Pub

Quilpie Railway Station

Paddy checking stock for TB

Paddy at Midkin

Paddy at Terachie

Alastair Bassingthwaighte

Bobby Lindores

Lighthouse at Blackall

Johnny Monoghan

Jackie Tully

Young Paddy with his dog

Paddy on horseback

Watering horses

Breakers at Charlotte Plains

Breakers at Charlotte Plains

Paddy Bourke

blowing a lot, he said to me, "What did you run away for?"

Neville came to us, "Let him go, Darcy. I'll look after him."

"No, I'll have to take him to the sergeant." Who was leaning against the fence with my hat.

"What did you run for?"

"I don't know."

"How old are you?" I said I was the legal age then Neville kept on saying to the Sarge that it was his fault and that he would look after me.

The Sarge asked me my age again and I said I was 18. He kept on asking me questions and again asked me my age. Sixteen, I said and with that he gave me my hat and with a grin said to Neville, "Better give him another drink and take him home. And you stay out of the pub and drink lemonade till you're 21."

With that Darcy speaks up and says, "And next time don't run 'cause I got to chase you."

It was one morning after that I was in the Metro and there was Hockey Dillon, the one-eye, and Jack Hudson - he was the brother of Billy, and Colin Cocks, the barman. We were drinking and the two of them started arguing. Hockey said he was going to kill Billy and Jacky said, "No, you won't."

"Yes, I will. I will belt the shit out of him next time he comes to town."

Jack said, "No, you won't."

With that Hockey said, "I'm the best man in this bar."

Jack said, "No, you're not. I am."

Hockey said, "Righto, out the back. And the best man shouts when we come back."

Jack said to Cockey, "Fill them up, we'll be back. Come on you," He grabbed me and said, "You can hold our shirts." We went down to what was called the Bull Ring, that's where they had all the big fights from the bar.

These two blokes weren't mates. Hockey Dillion was in the A.I.F. through the war and was a nice bloke if he liked you. I don't know where he was born but it was around St George. All the time I was there, he played football and was always sent in when his team was losing and Hockey sorted them out. When the two of them shaped up, Hockey was singing and grinning at the same time and it really got up Jack's nose.

I have seen a lot of fights around the pubs in my travels but I never saw anyone who could move on his feet like Hockey could. Hudson wanted to bury him or at least knock him out of the paddock. He was just skimming Hockey's chest – couldn't lay a hand on him. All Hockey kept on saying was, "No Jack, I don't want to hit you mate. You gave me five bob the other day so I don't want to hit you."

Hudson kept on saying, "Hit me you black bastard, 'cause I'll hammer you if I get you."

Hockey could have hit Jack any time he wanted to. It was one of the best spars I had ever saw. They broke it up without a hit being landed and we went back and started drinking again. I think Hockey just wanted to prove a point to Jack, and he did that.

There were a few in the bar when we went back and there was a bit of noise. We were standing at the end of the bar when Hockey started to sing a song about the A.I.F. It was unreal and he had a terrific sounding voice. I was right beside him, listening and watching him as he was staring straight ahead. I was on his blind side when all of a sudden he looked around at me, stopped singing and said, "What the – are you looking at?"

I said, "Nothing."

He went back to singing again. I can tell you, it frightened more than the proverbial out of me. There weren't too many fellows would have a go at Hockey.

Another time, there were half a dozen of us standing around a drum fire in Jacky Smith's garage. They ran the taxi cabs. We were yarning and having a drink when the sergeant and constable came in and the talk got around to Hockey Dillon. The sergeant said, "Why don't a couple of you double up on him, belt the shit out of him and if you kill him, you'll get off because he has such a bad name and reputation."

We all knew that he only wanted the locals to do what the police couldn't do. When Hockey came to town and got on the grog and started to play up, the police would come. Always two of them, and sometimes three. They would get him and always put the handcuffs on him to the back.

Eventually, I met up with a fellow around my age and he suggested we go to Mitchell Town up the Sandy Maranoa Ridge. So up we go and started looking for work. We were a bit young and not a lot of people wanted us because we didn't have the experience and couldn't handle young horses. We were put on to a drover looking for a couple of ringers. He was camped a couple of miles out of town so we got a taxi and out we go. When we get there we found the drover, Jerry, and he's black, not that there was anything wrong with that, just a bit unusual because there wasn't too many black fellows owned their own droving plant. He gave us the job and said he was leaving tomorrow for Mt Moffett Station, well over 100 miles up the Carnarvon Ranges so to be here the next morning with our gear.

The next morning we go out in the taxi again, get our gear out and let the taxi go. We went towards the wagonette and five bull terriers come out at us. So we stopped and they did the same. We sat under a tree just away from the camp and as long as we didn't attempt to go near the wagon, they did nothing. After an hour or so Jerry came back. He had been up to town to see the agents and said everything was right to go.

We were having a cup of tea and he saw I had my own saddle and wanted to know if I'd sell it to him.

I said, "Yes. £13."

He pulled his wallet out and paid me in cash - he had a lot of cash on him. He had his old mate with him, Reg, so there were four of us and off we go. We had a big wagonette and 40 horses. Every time we made camp he would catch fresh horses then get me to have a go at riding them. He didn't put me on anything real bad but they were all fresh and hadn't been worked for a while so would pigroot and play up.

We got up to a place called Womblebank Station and the wagonette did a bearing so Jerry said he would leave Les there. He could wait for the parts to come on the mail, fix it and have it ready for when we got back with the cattle.

"How far to go, Jerry?"

"Oh, just up the road, not far."

What an understatement. The next morning we get all these old pack saddles off the wagon. Jerry and Reg pack them with all the cooking gear and tucker we needed and I can tell you we never had much tucker. He got another young fellow to come with us - same age as us. We left around 7 am and we pulled up for a quick lunch, boiled our quart pots, had our corn loaf and damper and off again. He kept the mob of horses moving at a good pace.

When it became dark Jerry said he would go in the lead and for us to follow him. Right, we thought. So every time the horses went off the road, Jerry would throw one of his wax matches up the air and one of us would race up and turn the horses and that went on to late in the night.

It was pitch black so Jerry stopped the horses and told one of us to block them up. "Righto, grab a horse, then park it and take it's pack off over here."

That we did and he told me to light a fire.

"Where?" I said.

"Over at that bloody log of course."

I got the fire going and we were all buggered. So there was Jerry with three very tired boys. We were sitting on a log near the fire which was going real good by then. He was mixing up something when all of a sudden he says, "Here." And he threw something at me.

I caught it, looked at it and said, "What's this?"

"Throw it in the coals. That's your Johnny cake."

So we all did what he told us and with a cup of tea and a bit of meat, that was tea. I can tell you we were glad to go to bed that night. That was another first for me. All through the night you could hear the dingoes howling, very mournful sound. They sounded like they were all around us.

The next morning, while still very dark, Jerry wakes us all. We had a quick breakfast and he tells Colin and Billy to pack everything away while he and I went for the horses. He had them all in a cooler paddock he said. We packed up and were on our way again just on daybreak.

We travelled all day and finally got to Mt Moffett. The two boys stayed with the horses and Jerry took me with him. The boss came out to meet us on a horse, introduced himself and Jerry did the same. They had a bit of a yarn and then the boss, a Jimmy Walderon said, "Righto, we'll go down and count them over." It was something to see and hear. I will never forget it.

Jerry said, "What's today, Boss?"

"Friday. Why?"

"I'm not taking delivery today, make it in the morning."

Well, did Jimmy go off, "I got the bloody mob down there." We could see them and hear them. "I got my men holding them, have been since yesterday. I got other work to do."

But old Jerry just said, "Not today, Boss. Tomorrow." And tomorrow it was.

We still had a bit of daylight so we made a good camp. Jerry put me in charge of the horses. Colin was to be the cook and Billy was to be with Jerry. Jerry was the only man I'd seen drive the cattle the way he did. He had five bull terrier bitches, very good bitches, and he controlled them well. Also, I have never seen anyone else with a mob of dogs do what Jerry did. He would send one bitch say to the left wing then with a point of his whip handle and saying the dog's name, send one or two dogs to the right wing. With a crack of the whip and a whistle, he would point his horse whichever way or dog he was calling and that dog, or dogs, would come back and fall in behind his horse. The whole five of them would always run behind Jerry's horse and his horse only. Not like a lot of other dogs that I have seen, they run away and everywhere and behind anybody and horse.

One day, we were riding towards dinner camp and Jerry tapped a tree with his whip handle and said to the dogs, "Here, look at that goanna. Get the goanna." And the whole mob of dogs were going mad and jumping up and around the tree. Then just as quick he'd say, "That'll do."

When we got off our horses at dinner camp he says to his dogs, "Here, go away and play."

Pointing with the whip handle, all his dogs took off making a lot of noise and chasing each other. All except one who didn't seem to want to go - she stayed with his horse. Jerry just walked over to her, grabbed hold of her and flogged her with his whip, gave her a good hiding. Then said, "Now go and play."

That she did, took off flat out to the other dogs and when he was ready, he cracked his whip and they all came back.

Jerry told us that he was going to push the mob as he wanted to get back to Womblebank Station where the wagonette and his mate were. Anyway, he put the dogs into the cattle all day. They came out of dingo country so they knew what dogs were about. The first day on dinner camp they took off and it was something to see a mob of a thousand head of big bullocks flat out all going in the one direction. We blocked them up and he got into them again. That night he had a paddock to let them go into. It was used by the station to hold mobs in.

The second day was the same as the first. That night he got permission to use a set of old cattle yards. We could see the lights of the station. We had tea and were sitting on our swags around the fire. The cattle were pretty restless and making a lot of noise.

We were listening to Jerry telling us some old bush tales when he said, "Why don't you boys take your swags up to that big box tree near the yards, light a good fire and keep it going through the night. That might settle them down."

So we did. All three of us lit a good fire and rolled our swags out. We had the fire between us and the tree and then the cattle. We were all tired so we were ready for sleep. We were laughing and joking and going on when all of a sudden there was a loud crack. A rail of the yard broke we reckon. Then, as if you had control over all the cattle and you could throw a switch to shut the noise off, everything went quiet, not a sound.

I said to the boys, "You see that fork in the tree? If they go I will be the first one there." Just joking.

Then Colin, or Lance as he was going under two names, said, "You know the old saying?"

"What?" We asked.

"A calm before a storm," he said.

There wasn't any noise coming from the yards and it sounded and felt real spooky when all of a sudden all hell broke loose. The cattle busted the yards and they were rushing, making a hell of a noise bellowing and mooing and we could hear the timber breaking. It was a lot of box country, very thick with a lot of suckers. When they first took off I thought I was quick getting out of my swag and running to the big tree but when I got to the fork, the other two were there before me. There we were, the three of us all singing out, "Whoa cattle, whoa boys,"

Jerry was doing the same. We went back to where he was and he wasn't real happy. He blamed us for starting them and was right up us but he had to have someone to blame and wasn't going to blame himself. So who better to blame but three young fellows.

The next morning I had the horses at camp real early. We all packed up and were waiting for daylight so as we could see the muster and also see what the damage was. The cocky and his men came to the camp. The cocky was getting up Jerry and I heard him say, "Well, you can pay to fix the yards and the fences too."

They gave us a hand to muster the mob. I can't recall how many we lost but I do recall cattle dead in the yards and there were the ones with broken shoulders and knocked off horns – bloody awful to see. The cocky shot the ones that were crippled. That was my first stampede or rush, as they call them. Unreal.

When we got to Womblebank Station everyone knew about what had happened and of course, Jerry was still blaming us. I wouldn't accept the blame and he was going to put the dogs on me and Colin. I really think if there hadn't been a couple of ringers from the station there, he would have done just that. So I said I wasn't going any further with him and that turned him on again. So both Colin and me took our swags off the wagonette and got a taxi out of Mitchell. A fair way it was, 9d a mile – we didn't care.

Jerry paid us by cheque. I thought that strange for when he paid me for my saddle he had a wallet full of five and ten pound notes. We had two weeks' pay. Colin had £11 and I had £13 so when we got to town the taxi owner said he couldn't cash a cheque and to pay him later at the cafe where his stand was. So we headed over to Hughy Lemons' store to buy some new clothes and whatever where Hughy added it all up. We had our ration book and Identity Card. He asked us who Jerry was.

"Oh, he's a boss drover coming in with a mob of Mt Moffett - going to truck them here."

So that was alright until he looked at Colin's cheque and it had Lance Allen on it. Mine had my right name on all three. He looked at us and said, "I'll cash this one." Mine.

"And you can cash the other at the bank." So that worked out all right but we still had to pay for the taxi.

As we was walking up the main street of Mitchell, the bank manager bailed us up and asked if we were the two ringers that was with the mob from Mt Moffett. We said yes, and he wanted to know all about what had happened and where Jerry was now. We told him and that was that. We weren't game to give him Colin's cheque so we went to the cafe and had a good meal and gave the lady the cheque. We told her to take the cost of the trip and meals from it.

The next day when we went back to the café, didn't the lady give it to us. Called us everything that wasn't nice. That was because the cheque bounced. We told her the truth; we didn't know that the cheque was no good and that it was a wage cheque. She believed us and was alright after that. As soon as Jerry got to town and trucked the mob, the bank put a hold on him and seized his plant. After a period of time, they sold him up. I don't know what happened to him after that.

It was winter time and very cold. They had a rodeo at the trucking yards. They bucked the horses into a rope round yard – big yard at that. I had a ride and did no good. We were told there was a drover there looking for a couple of ringers. We found him and asked him for a job. He said no, that he was right for men. While we were talking to him and another bloke, this young fellow came out of the chute on a rough horse. The horse fell over and lay on the ground – they had run the horse out. The bloke got up and fell straight down again, kicking and moving around a lot. The ambulance chap raced in and held on to him. When the young fellow settled he got up and the ambo told him he just had a fit and he thought it a good time for him to go home. So his mate, who was talking to the drover, took off out of the yards. We started to walk away when the drover sang out to us. He knew who we were and said he did have a job but only for one. Couldn't say anything before because the other two were looking for a job and he didn't want to put them on. So I took the one job and I never ran into Colin again. That was in 1947.

The drover had a mob of Mt Taylor bullocks. This time there were only 500 fats heading for NSW. The boss was Jack Towsen and he had his father, Jack, with him who was in his late 50s or early 60s. And a big fellow, Les Fuller, a real nice and very quiet bloke who sort of looked after me. I picked them up the next day south of Mitchell and heading for St George. The cattle had been on the road for a while and were quiet to handle and had settled into the routine of droving.

As we got down the road some, Jack said we were going to run into some dry days as a few of the dams had dried up and we had to rely on the waterholes in the Maranoa River. We were going along fine until we came to the no water days. We were going through sandy pine tree country, pretty rough and thick and full of rabbits and there were warrens everywhere.

The first day was dry and the cattle were restless. The men said that I could do the dog watch and they would split the rest of the night into three. So while they were having their tea I was out on watch riding around singing to them. Around about 8 pm they all hit their feet and took off. Jack yelled out to me to bring the horse to him. He took off in the night and you could hear Les cooeeing out and Jack following him. After a fair while they had the cattle back on camp and they had very little sleep that night.

I was doing cooking so was driving my first wagonette only with two horses. Les would give me a hand to the next camp, hobble the horses out and then go back to the cattle and give the two Jacks a hand. We had stages like that. The mob would go a day and night and water on the next day, usually late. They were long days and so they had to push them along a bit.

The cattle were doing what the Mt Moffatt mob were doing; they were rushing on dinner camp and in the night. They took a couple of fences along the way and were getting a bad name. Every night Jack would call me in early. The cattle got that predictable that as they said, you could just about set your watch by them. One night I was sound asleep in my swag and I woke up, singing out and climbed up a pine tree. And sure enough the mob was rushing. When I came down out of the tree my feet were both full of dog burr and wasn't I sore after that night.

Then one morning around 1 am, I woke up and Jack and his father were having a very heated argument with a cocky who was drunk. He was telling Jack to get the mob off his boundary netting fence. Jack told him to go to buggery and the cocky said, "If you don't shift them, then I will. I'll drive the bastards off with my ute."

With that threat, Jack sang out to me, "Quick, throw me down the rifle." And I got him the .303 army rifle. Jack loaded in front of the cocky and told him that if he drove anywhere near the mob that he'd blow his ute to pieces. That put the wind up the cocky and he took off home.

The next day they had 17 miles or better and we were told that there was a new Government dam and that it was full. By the time I caught up to the mob, they had to let them go as the cattle got the smell of water and they couldn't hold them back. They were going to get close to the dam and then cut them in and water them that way.

Jack came over to me and said, "There's an exchange down the road. Go there and give notice to the following properties." He gave me a list of dates and names.

"While you're there, ask them if they saw or heard of any cattle."

So when I got to the phone exchange, I think it was called 'over flow', I did what I was told and then asked the lady about the cattle. She looked at me and laughed and said, "Go down a mile or so and you'll come to the big dam. You'll find them all down there."

When I did get to the dam it was unreal to see them. There were cattle everywhere – swimming, drinking and just lying around. The boys got to that dam before dinner, put them into a mob, counted them and found them all there. Jack was going to have a day's spell but that night it rained and his worries were over as far as water was concerned.

We had a good trip all the rest of the way; good feed, plenty of water and then we got rain. It was very boggie all along the stock route. I could handle two horses in harness but when we got to south of Thallow, Jack yolked up four and I was getting into trouble with them. So Jack took them over, gave me his horse to ride and I went with the cattle.

The last words young Jack said to me were, "Dad will try and tell you what to do but he's not your boss, I am. You stay on the tail and just keep them moving. And if he does start giving you orders, tell him to get well nicked. I'll be back as soon as I set the camp up for you."

Everything went well for the morning. We had just come through a gate and Les and old Jack were having a smoke and old Jack told me to get around to the wing. I answered back to him that I would stay where I was, on the tail. He got very upset, called me a cheeky young bastard and said he'd knock me off the horse. Then I told him he wasn't my boss, young Jack was. With that he jammed the spurs into his horse and came galloping towards me and he meant it too. I waited until he was right on top of me, then I jumped off my horse and, quick as I could, turned my horse's rump into his horse. It shied away and he nearly came off his horse. Just then young Jack turns up and says, "What's going on here?"

Old Jack tells him I gave him a lot of cheek and adds a lot more to it. Next thing I know young Jack is on one side of me, old Jack on the other side of me and the both of them wanting to fight me. I said I could fight the two of them but I would have a go at young Jack.

"You young bastard. Get your swag off my wagon and go to buggery but get."

With that I told him, "You put it on, you pull it off."

That's when big Les came over, got off his horse and said, "Leave the kid alone. If you want to fight, have a go at me." With that they both went to water.

I told Jack that I'd go as far as Mungindi, that was another five or six days to go. When we got into the NSW side of Mungindi, I told Jack I was leaving him. He didn't say anything to me, just wrote my cheque out. I said, "Thanks, but you remember, Jack, I won't always be as small as I am now and I'll meet you again one day and knock your bloody head off." He just laughed but I made sure that Les was there when I said it.

I worked with Les some years later and I did run into Jack some years later too. But that's another story.

It was only about a hundred miles or better to St George so I went on a mail truck and headed for there again. Pop was still there on his own, the boys had left and poor old Paddy O'Connor was in hospital. Pop was glad to see me. He asked me what I had been doing and when I told him about the two wanting to fight me he laughed and thought it a great joke. I was walking down the main street and old Bill Lindores stopped to ask me why I left and I told him. He was only paying me boys' wages and that I had been getting men's wages everywhere else I had been. So he asked me would I come back with him if he paid me full wages and I said yes. I was glad I did because he was a nice old fellow and I had a lot of good times and laughs with him. I stayed with old Bill for three years and only left him in 1950 when there was a big flood on.

We were out at one place called Kooroon and we were all living in the main house, a high set house, as they had no living quarters there. One morning they got this .303 rifle out and was mucking about with it. I asked Colin Lindores, a son of Bill's, "Can I have a shot?"

"Yeah. Here, shoot at the drum," he said. Then he said, "No. Here, come up here."

I had loaded the gun and was about to shoot when he stopped me. Colin grabbed the barrel near the end of the gun and he was walking me up to the other end of the verandah.

"See that old tank over there?" And he was pointing to it.

I had my finger on the trigger and while walking with him, I was all tensed up. I didn't realise it but I was squeezing the trigger slowly but firmly. I answered yes and just as I did, the gun went off with a hell of a bang. Colin jumped and let the gun go. I got such a fright I let the gun go and it hit the floor. Everybody else was laughing and shouting. It ended up a big joke but as old Bill said, lucky I didn't shoot somebody. That was my first shot of a .303.

We went down to a shed called Oakey Park. The owner, Ned Hill, would let us go pig shooting on the weekends – there were pigs everywhere. I bought myself my first rifle, a .303. It would kick like a mule.

CHAPTER SEVEN

One weekend it rained very heavy and we got flood bound – couldn't go anywhere or do anything. So we stayed in the hut for more than a week. There were three of us, Kerry Fields, Colin Lindores and me.

One day I came out of my room along the verandah going to the kitchen. You had to step down the two steps, turn right and step up two to get in the kitchen. Just as I touched the ground, going to turn right, Colin came running out of the kitchen and had my rifle. He pointed at my feet and said, "Dance, you bastard, dance."

I was standing feet apart as there was a pool of water near the step and you had to take a wide step to get over it. As soon as I saw the rifle I just looked at him and told him to go and get nicked. With that he pulled the trigger and the gun went off with a hell of a bang. Water splashed up all over my legs and I can tell you, I danced alright. But it was all in fun - we were going mad from having nothing to do.

Another year at the same shed, we were shearing and it was winter time. It was that cold there that the bore drain used to stop flowing. It ran past the shed and the huts. We would go out in the morning and break the ice on top and you would see the water running underneath the ice. So what the cook would do every night before going to bed, was to put two kerosene tins of water beside the open fire and when he got up early in the morning he would bank them over the fire. So when all the men got up we would have warm water to wash with. There were eleven men in the team and it was something everybody did – have a wash before going to the table.

Well, that first weekend came and we said we would stay on the station. So before the other men took off on Friday afternoon they asked us if we wanted anything from town and we all decided on getting some wine. I got two bottles of Muscatel, 2s 6d a bottle, very cheap and black. It was to be only for a drink before tea. When the men returned on Sunday they were pretty tanked and as usual, up to no good. They got myself and Allan, who we call the Gatton Gorger because of what and how he ate his meals, they got us on the wine, or plonk as we knew it. It wasn't long before we were really drunk.

Prior to all this I had overheard one of the shearers saying, "Look at the dirty bastard. Hasn't had his coat off for a decent wash since we've been here." They were talking about this yellow fellow, Billy Clemens, a shearer from St George. Not a good one but flat out doing 120 sheep a day. He was known as a bad bugger as he'd killed his father, so it was said.

Everyone was standing around the fire having a talk and telling yarns and somehow they got the two of us sparring up to each other. It was just on dark. Black Billy had his back to us and was facing the fire, had his hands clasped behind.

I don't know what made me do it (had to be the grog) but I bounced up to him and said, "You black bastard. Haven't had your coat off since you've been here. I'll make you take it off."

I hit him behind the ear. His knees buckled, he bounced back up, jumped the plank, ripped his coat off and said, "You young bastard. I'll give you a fight." And came towards me.

I was still bouncing around and didn't have any fear of him but for Bobby Lindores he would have really trashed me. I can recall Bobby saying to him, "You were quite happy being party to the boys getting drunk, so put up with it."

Somebody put me to bed that night and the next morning I had my breakfast and walked over to the shed. Bobby came to me, told me what I had done and said, "You better go and apologise to Billy and tell him you're sorry." That I did. I could see he was still not happy but he said, "That's alright boy, forget it."

As soon as they started shearing, I ran outside and started heaving my heart up. They took me into the wool room and for the next two days I laid on the wool bales getting over it – very sick. Everybody ribbed me for it. Once I got over it I swore that I would never drink wine again. I have been to a lot of weddings and parties and to this day, can't bring myself to even sip or have a taste of any drink that has to do with wine.

It was the following week and I was back to normal again and I was learning to shear. I was coming down the long blow of the sheep and Billy was bent over in front of me. He was loading his machine, getting ready to start. So I did to him what the other shearers had done to me, as a joke. When you are bent over your pants become tight. You're busy doing what you're doing and the shearer who is behind you reaches out with his hand piece and lays it flat on your rump. It vibrates real fast, doesn't hurt but because you're not expecting it, gives you a hell of a fright. My first time, I jumped into the counting out pen and that frightened the shearer, Ronny Mitchell more than it did me.

There was Billy's butt in front of me and I just couldn't help it - I put the machine onto his butt. Well, he jumped and sang out real loud and dropped his machine, which was engaged at the time. His machine was jumping all over the floor - they really do bounce and real quick. Someone pulled his machine out of gear and all hell broke loose again. What I thought was a joke, and a good one at that, turned into trouble for me. Billy pulled my machine out of gear and I let the sheep that I was shearing go. It was racing all around the board until somebody grabbed it. Billy was roaring at me, calling me everything that he could and was going to knock my head off again. Once again, Bobby stepped in between us and gave Billy another talking to. Told him that it's alright when he did it, but no good when it happened to him.

"Leave the kid alone. If you want to have a go at anybody, have a go at me." And with that the incident was over.

Bobby told me, "You keep away from him. He won't be happy until he gets at you." So I did just that.

It was two weeks later, we were all in town and the St George Rodeo was on at the weekend. The horses were bucking well and the cattle better. Billy Clemens came out on a big rough bullock. He was riding it well and right at the end of his ride of eight seconds, his whip cracked and the whistle blew at the same time. So he was disqualified. But just as he fell off, the beast kicked him in the ear. The ambulance went out and took him to the hospital. They told us over the speakers that he was dead and believe me, that never upset me at all. That was around 1949.

It was in 1950 in the middle of the year that my life took another turn. We had a big flood, water everywhere. No one could go anywhere. All the roads were dirt in those days. The only road out of St George was the built up road to Thallow and Mungindi. Kerry Fields and Don Pengilly, both from NSW, said, "Let's go to Sydney."

Kerry had a good Model T Ford ute. So we went and told Bill what we were about and he said okay, so long as we were back when they started shearing again and that wouldn't be for a week or more. So we threw our gear in the back and set off for Sydney. We got as far as five miles south of Mungindi and couldn't go any further as the road and bridges were all washed out and impassable. So we went back and put the ute onto a train and we went down by the mail train.

We got to Sydney and Kerry wanted to go and see his sister who was living and working there. Donny wanted to do the same. We had a good hour or more to wait for the train going to St Mary's where Kerry's parents lived. His dad had a shoe repairing shop, and a good one at that. So I was to stay with Kerry and we would all meet back at Sydney Central. I couldn't get over the size of the city and how many people were there.

We saw Kerry's sister and we had to hurry back to the station. As we ran through the gate the guard who was minding our gear sang out to us, "Hey, you fellows want this train?"

We sing out, "Yes."

"Well, move yourselves. Quick, get in here."

So we grab all our gear and while he was holding the door open for us, the train started to move. We threw all the gear in, jumped in and the guard slammed the door shut and gave the signal to the train guard. We were hanging out the windows and saw Donny come flying through the gate. He was running very fast but the guard stopped him and we sang out, "See you in St Mary's." He had Kerry's address and knew his way.

We got to Kerry's place and I met his mum and dad – real nice. They gave us lunch and after that showed me their spare room and it was full of their loose gear. Later on Kerry wanted to go to the only pub that was there to see his mates. So we got a cab and down we go. When all his friends saw him they went mad. They wouldn't let either of us shout a drink. Around 5 pm all the workers came rushing in and they would order four or five pints of beer.

I saw them just tip the glass and in two goes it was gone and they would be back for more. I was getting near to being full by this time but still recall saying to Kerry,

"I want one of them." Pointing to a bloke near me who had just had three of them and did it easily. So he got one and gave it to me.

I still don't know if I finished it or not but the next thing I hear someone yelling out, "Time, gents, time."

It was only just 6 o'clock by me so I started banging on a bit, saying, "It's not ten and I'm not going."

After everyone else had left they just came up to us and luckily for me Kerry knew them and said he would look after me. So they put us outside and shut the door behind us. It was pouring down rain and we had nowhere to shelter. So Kerry left me to get a cab.

I wasn't used to the NSW beer and when they turfed me out and the fresh air hit me, I really lost it. Didn't know where I was and didn't care. The pub was on the main road to Sydney and Penrith. There I was having a technicolour chuck, lying down, water pouring off me and all the cars going by blowing their horns and singing out. But I was too sick to care. Kerry came back with a cab and we went to his place. I didn't want to go in and told Kerry to bring my swag out and I was going to camp outside under the shop front. Next thing I know Mrs Field was there insisting I come inside and get dressed into dry clothes. She put me in the bathroom, gave me a towel and had a pair of pyjamas and dressing gown when I came out. She sat me down at a lovely meal and took me out to the spare room. She opened the door and I couldn't believe it – all cleaned out with a big double bed and three pillows. By this time Donny had caught up to us so we stayed there for a week until we got a job.

Then Donny and I moved into Ma's Boarding House, the only one in St Mary's, a rough old bitch. We did play up but nothing bad. One day we came home and she had all our gear outside in a heap and a big lock on the door. We had nowhere to go so Mrs Fields took us back again. We went to the police and told them what really happened and how she turfed us out. They wrote it all down and checked our weekly rent receipt and said that we weren't the only ones that she had done this to. And the way she wrote the receipt out showed as though we were a week behind. So it was a good experience to have again.

Mrs Fields got us into one of their friend's place on the Nepean River at Emu Plains just past Penrith. She made the two of us promise that we would behave ourselves. She took us out to meet the people. The place was called Hunting Hall Guest House. It was a holiday resort for the business people. They said they were going to take in 10 boys and 10 girls. They charged us a very reasonable rate and said we weren't allowed to tip the staff and that we would be served in turn.

You name it, they had it! Rowing, fishing, golf, tennis, horses, snooker and they had a dance hall. We danced every Saturday night. They drove us to the station and picked us up after work. Cooked our dinners and treated us like they did the business people. We mixed and got on real well. I worked out of St Mary's for nearly six months until I got paint down my guts – made me very sick. So I left and headed back for good old Queensland.

I headed back to St George and went shearing with a contractor at Bollon, 72 miles west of St George. I was what they termed a learner and when you shear your first 100 sheep then they say you're a shearer. I shore my first 100 at a place called Binda owned by an arsehole named Bill Moody. None of the old shearers liked him.

One day, he came racing up the board to my stand screaming out to me to pull the wool off. The Rep came down to see what he was going on about. He said, "He's leaving the wool around the crutch."

The Rep jumped down my pen and came back with a small hand full of wool. "Is this what you're getting upset about?"

Moody said, "Yes".

"Well, go and have a look down my pen and you'll see a lot more than this. So if you want your sheep shorn, get off the board and leave the young fellow alone or we'll walk."

So as he was going I said to him, "There's enough wool down all the shutes to buy yourself a whip. Buy one as it would look good on you." That went down like a rock.

We finished the shed with no more trouble and headed for Bollon, the one pub town. We got on the grog as per usual on the Saturday. We were running a bit short of money. I said to my two mates, "Berty is in town. He owes me twenty quid. I'll go and bone him for it."

I found him in the store next to the pub. I asked him for some of the money he'd owed me and for quite a time too. He told me, "I owe you nothing, now get lost."

With that I told him it was worth that much to know him. I turned to walk away when all of a sudden, bang! He hit me a beauty right on the jaw. It spun me right around and I was facing him again.

"Now go and get your mates 'cause I got mine."

One of my mates was a yellow fellow name of Sidney Love, fought like mad and loved it. We ended up in the bar and a real shit stirrer, Tom Bradford, was working in the shed for the opposition - big fellow. Sidney was going to take him on. It was getting fairly heated and the publican called the police.

Up came the sergeant, settled it all down and said, "Right you three, down to the station." So he walked us down and he had hold of my two mates, put them inside the gate and stood there waiting for me to catch up.

"Come on, get a move on." I could feel his boot as I passed him. He took our names and ages. I was 18 and he told me to stay out of the pubs and drink lemonade until I was 21.

"And if I catch you in here again, look out."

Not long after that episode I was in town on the weekend, not drinking, and this married couple who I knew from the shearing sheds, came up to me and asked if I knew of anyone with a car as they wanted to get out to Castle Vale Station about 13 miles out of Bollon. They were pretty drunk and it was late in the afternoon. So I went and saw this old fellow, Bill Turvey. He was in the bar, drunk. I asked him for a loan of his truck a 1927 Chev. It had a big flat top tray on it as Bill used to do fencing for old Story Winks, a good old grazier. Bill would always give me his truck but not this day. He said he would drive them out himself. So I went and got May and Ray Alldridge and another ringer from the same place, we got on the truck and out we go.

All Bill could keep on saying and repeating over all the way out was, "I just turned 70 today and I feel real well."

"Yes, Bill," I would say. I was sitting on his right so the tray of the truck came out alongside of the driver's seat.

They had just graded the main road and it was wide – all dirt road and dusty. Old Bill would go to one side and I would turn the truck back to the middle of the road. By the time we got out to the 10 mile gate, it was getting on to dark. Bill was driving a bit fast and I told him we were coming up to the turn off but too late. He turned the wheel and we were heading for a thick clump of gidyea trees. So I jumped up and was going to lay flat on the back on the floor of the truck and the next thing I could feel myself floating through the air. I felt no pain or anything until I woke up and I heard one of them saying and singing out to the others, "Hey, here he is over here." He grabbed me by my arm to roll me over and that's when I came to with the pain.

They tell me the truck was wrecked so they had to walk to the station for help. When they got there they were still drunk and noisy. Had to wake the owner up. This time it was late in the night and the owner, who knew me, would not give them his good car to take me into town. He said they could take the Overlander ute – very rough to ride in.

The next thing I remember was lying on a bed and I heard the Matron saying to the sergeant, "I don't like it sergeant. I think it's an operation and I can't do that here."

I woke up, opened my eyes and was looking straight at the sergeant. He asked me how I felt and if I had any drink. I said, "No."

He patted me on the arm and said, "You'll be right."

Next I remember I was in an ambulance, heading for the St George Hospital. I pulled them up twice along the way and had a throw up. The next thing I know it's daylight and a nurse was slapping me and calling out my name. She threw some cold water on my neck and that really woke me up! They found out who I was and got in contact with Pop who came up to see me. I was alright and he laughed, cracked a few jokes, said I'd get over it and he left me. He said he was going to see his old mate, Paddy O'Connor, who had taken real sick. So when I was well enough, I would go and sit with Paddy. He got so sick they took him to Brisbane General and he died there from silicosis. Pop said it was dust on the lungs and he had it from working in the mines.

I was in hospital for nearly a week and every morning, when Dr McDonald and Matron came round, I would ask if I could get out of bed and he would say, "No, not yet. You're too crook."

So one day, I got out of bed and went to where they kept our clothes. I wrapped them in a towel and went to the river, changed my clothes and walked to town. I borrowed five pounds from Jack Smith - he was one of the taxi owners and he had heard of my accident. Late in the evening I would get Jack to take me back to the hospital. All the nurses knew what I was doing and said if the doctor found out I would be in trouble. I did this for a week and I went to the pictures on the Saturday night.

The next day, when they were doing their rounds, the doctor did the usual and asked me how I was. Before I could ask him if I could get out of bed again, the matron speaks up and says, "Well, Doctor, this young man was at the picture show last night."

The doctor looked at me real hard and asked, "Is that right?"

I said, "Yes."

He checked me over and then said, very sternly, "If that's the way you feel, you can get dressed and I'll discharge you now. But you're a very silly boy and, one day, you will suffer for your stupidity. Now go and get dressed!"

I left St George, went back to Bollon and went out to a shed, crutching. I could only do around 350 sheep a day and found it too hard on me and gave the sheds away, never to go shearing again. That really changed my life again.

I got drunk in Bollon on New Years Eve, 1951. I got on the mail lorry, lay in the hot sun all day and got to Cunnamulla in the afternoon. The driver went straight to the Post Office which was next to the Police Station. I threw my swag and port on the road and left it there. I walked across to the Cockies Pub – that's where all the nobs and graziers stayed – and asked if they had a room.

The look was enough, she said, "No, try down the road."

So I went to what they called Bronwyn's Pub. The barmaid took one look at me and asked if I wasn't feeling well. I told her I was just about dead. She laughed and gave me a bed in Room 7. I had to walk back up to the Post Office and my gear was still there on the road. I got back to the pub, lay on the bed and watched the iron ring they used for mosquito net attached to the bed-head. It was bouncing in time with my heartbeat.

I got over that bout and got a job in a place called Charlotte Plains, owned by Gordon Nagell and his good wife. She was really good to me. She put me in charge of the horses and I did all the maintenance on all their machinery. Gordon would always come alive around four in the afternoon, or later, and drink all night. He played cards for money with a lot of the business people from town. About 35 miles out, they would come out and get on the rum supplied by Gordon. I got to know where he kept it as I helped the mailman unload all the stores one day, and put it in his room, which was beside the office.

One day I was returning the key to the fuel shed. I was standing there waiting for Roy Walsh, the bookkeeper, to come and I noticed the lock was the same. I quickly tried it and it worked. Just then, Roy came and said, "Yes, Paddy, can I help you?"

I asked him if he had any mail and he said, "No," so I walked off and kept the key. That night, at about 10 pm, when all the boys were asleep, I went over, got into the room and found his rum and knocked off two bottles of Blue Jackett. A nice rum it was. I used to knock off and drink around six bottles a week. He didn't miss it for a while because he got it in a case, four dozen at a time.

All this time while we were drinking, someone had come out with trucks and had stolen a number of sheep from the property. You could see where they had loaded them on to the trucks. The police decided to put on a muster to find out how many had been stolen.

We mustered and counted the main paddock and found the numbers down by around 500. So they decided to muster all the sheep on the main roads. It turned out to be a disaster as the ewes were about to lamb. They lost a lot of lambs by doing it that way but that's what the police wanted. During the muster the cops slept in the big house.

One night old Harry Haysman, the handyman come gardener, and me get into Harry's old truck, a KB5 ute. We got our rum and off we went up to the bore paddock eight miles out. That's when old Jack Emblen, one of the last bullock drivers, lived on the bore drain. We got on the rum and had a good night.

About 1 am in the morning, Harry and I headed home with me driving. The truck had no muffler and was very noisy. I drove into the courtyard and with the noise of the truck and old Harry, woke everyone up. Out came the cop known as Baby Face in town – he's up us. Said he came out to work and not to be annoyed by bloody drunks, he got enough of them in town.

We only laughed and Harry said, "And what do you think you are going to do?"

The cop said, "If you both don't get to bed, I'll lock youse up." With that old Harry burst out laughing at him. You could see the cop's face changing. Just then Mrs Haysman came up to us, grabbed Harry by his other arm and we took him to bed. Boy, what a night that was.

I was at Charlotte Plains for about six months and decided to move on. I got on real well with Mrs Nagell and when I told her I was going she got really upset and said to wait until Gordon, who was down in Sydney to see his horse race, came home. But I had enough of drinking his rum. It got to the stage where I was knocking off six bottles of his Blue Jacket rum a week. I went to a bit of trouble to cover it up but old Harry used to just go to his fridge and help himself. He had half empty bottles all around the station homestead.

Mrs Nagell wanted to know the reason for me going and I told her that when I came here I was run down from being on the road droving. I had the barcoo rot bad – you get it from rough tucker and not having any greens or vegetables. And you get pusy sores all over your arms and hands.

"I have been here on good tucker and I am well again. I have had a good holiday and I am ready for work. And if you know of anyone who is run down and in need of a holiday, tell them to get a job on Charlotte Plains and they will get over all their problems."

She said she liked my honesty and knew what I meant. She gave me a real good, strong handshake, one of the best I had had from a woman and one of only three in my time. She said if I ever wanted to come back just give her a ring. I was later to work on all four of their properties.

I went to town for a while and did the usual – got on the grog. Met a lot of nice people in Cunnamulla , did some horse breaking and went back droving again.

CHAPTER EIGHT

Somehow I ended up in Charleville and was drinking in the old Dalton Pub. It had just burnt down a couple of months back and they put up a small temporary bar on the block. It was opposite the Charleville Pub that was owned by old Harry Corones, who also owned the big hotel in town called Corones Hotel.

I was in the Charleville bar and I met this long legged ringer. Started drinking with him and he said that his dad was looking for a man to go on the road droving and if I was interested to come on home and meet him. That was my first meeting of one of the nicest families I had ever met in the bush, and I had met a few in my travels. My drinking mate was around my age and his name was Bob. Bobby Castles lived with his mum and dad. She was a lovely lady and he was a real top bloke. His name was George Castles and his wife's name was Gwen. You would go a long way to meet a family like them. Their other boys were there and I met them. There was Benny and then there was their daughter, Ellen, still going to school - a real fiery one. And one to teach anybody how to drive a mob of bullocks in a team, but really nice and properly spoilt. Then came Les who got called a lot of names later going to school so his mum called him The Galloping Ghan because he was always in a hurry and cantering his horse.

I started with George and Benny the next day. We mustered their horses, packed the big wagonette and left for Almena Station out from Whyandra. It turned out that George had been doing most of their cattle droving for years. Almena was owned by the Smith Brothers – nice people. They looked after us whenever we went to their property. It took us three days to get there and we camped on the bore drain near the cattle yards. I was horse tailing for George.

That was the start of a good friendship that I have had for many years. But, I must say, I had never seen a family argue over who had the best dog or horse or saddle! We used to do a lot of horse-breaking and put the young horses in the droving plant – best ever education for any young ones.

My first ever trip with George was to Wyandra trucking yards with 500 head of fats from Alimena Station. We had three young foals broke in and one chestnut mare; very smart and quick on her feet - could and would root too. Was going real good when all of a sudden, she got hard to catch. Ben and I spent a good couple of hours chasing her around the mob, trying every trick we knew. We finally caught her out of a tree. I got up this gidgee tree and Ben worked the mare, Topsy, around until she was beneath me. I hit the mare with the rope and caught her first up – you really only get one go at that. I put a hobble-strap on and a chain to the other front leg and drove her to the dinner camp.

Ben and I went back to give his dad, George, a hand with the mob. When we got to him he was sitting on his horse, looking at us, and could see that Topsy had been playing up. Ben speaks up and says what she had done and how we caught her and how she had bucked when I had got onto her. He told George about the chain on her and says she won't do that again. Old George just looked at us and says,

"You won't want to do that again or you're sacked." Then he looked at me and said, "The pair of you!"

He was a very good stockman and good at what he did. The best drovers were never short of work. Ben and I did a lot of trips with him. He had a good mob of horses and looked after them well. He had a big thoroughabrace wagonette. One trip, we finished at the Wyandra Trucking Yards and the bullocks were that fat that they busted the loading ramp while we were trucking them. The railway had to fix them straight away as there were other mobs behind us and they couldn't truck until the repairs had been done.

After trucking, George went and did what he always did – over to the pub and paid us, had a drink or two then rang his wife, Gwen, who would be at work by that time. This time he got a message that Gwen was at the hospital with their only daughter, Ellen, who was very sick. So we quickly mustered the horses, yoked up the wagon and off we set for home, some 70 miles by the stock route. We got home just on dark and Ben and I had the horses picked up and he and his dad went to the hospital to see Ellen. She was very sick but got over that to face a lot worse in the years to come. We came all that way in one day and the horses never stressed, apart from the ones Ben and I rode. They hardly raised a sweat. We changed the wagon and our mounts four times on the trip.

We headed back to Alimena Station for another mob. This time, when we got there, the boys got a big brown snake in the showers and another one in one of their bedrooms. They were really stirred up. This was mainly because their hut was built beside the bore drain and that was overgrown with grass and other matter.

I never used to keep a day horse; just let the mob go and find their spot to feed on. They were a good mob of horses; kept together and, as long as the feed was around, wouldn't walk far. Every time I went for the horses on foot, late of an afternoon, I would carry my bridle and mainly catch the old wagon mare, Dolly, as she was quiet and fat, easy to ride bare-back. On my way back to the camp I would nearly always look down and see a big brown snake lying where only a few minutes ago I had been walking.

I would always say to Benny, "Bugger that, I am keeping a horse tomorrow." But I never did.

One afternoon Ben and I were having a cup of tea around the camp fire and we heard this cart horse with a bell on it jump around and shake its head.

Ben said, "What's wrong with him?"

I said, jokingly, "Probably bitten by a brown!"

Sure enough, when I went down to get them that afternoon, the horse was dead, bitten on the lip. Old George said it was his first horse he had lost to a snake bite. That put the willys up me after that.

I had a spell from droving with old George and went back ringing. Ended up on a place on the Cunnamulla Road, 35 miles from Charleville, called Delilah; owned by the Nagells. They had Guy Nanties managing it – a nice bloke and easy to work for. He wanted me to break in a few horses and help do the mustering. It was a real nice property – right on the Warrego River, had some good fishing holes right near the homestead.

This is the place where I met the one and only one John David Monaghan. Came from Deacon, Brizzy. We got to be mates and got on really well. Johnny had a Matchless motorbike and I had a Tiger 100 Trumpy so we had something in common! I was there for a couple of weeks, had a quid and said to Monaghan,

"Come on, we'll go into town." Meaning Charleville.

All he would say was, "No, let's go to Whyandra."

I told him it was a shit hole, nothing there, only one pub and tough cop named Frank Grace.

"No, I don't know anybody in Charleville." Was what he would say. Anyway, I told him I would introduce him to the Castle family.

"You'll like them and we will go to the dance." And that did it.

So come Saturday morning we strapped our swags to the back of our bikes and headed off. We got to George and Gwen's early, around 8.30 am. Never forget it. Just as we pull up there was Winnie, one of Gwen's sisters, who lived next door, and Marie Birch, one of Gwen's nieces who was living in a big tent out front of Gwen's front fence. She was with her husband and one kid called Biddy, a lovely baby. Just as we stopped our bikes and lent them over on the jip stand, Marie comes out of Winnie's house and the language was something to hear. They were both at it and it was very strong. Not too many men would use it the way that these two ladies did. I looked at Johnny and could see the look on his face.

I said, "Don't take any notice, you'll get used to that."

That was Monaghan's introduction to the Castles and to his change of life in and around Charleville. From that weekend on we always took off on our bikes to Charleville. Johnny had been on Delillah Station around three years or more and that's all he knew.

We were sent down to Kenersley Station, John and I, to bring back a small mob of cattle. Had to truck them at Murweh Siding. We only camped out the one night and pitched our camp right on the banks of the Warrego River. It was pretty cold through the night. We kept the camp fire going all night (I did anyway). Johnny always liked his bed and you always had to wake him. But this night because it was cold, very cold, we had a heavy frost and Johnny was up sitting at the fire and singing out for me to get out of bed. So I laid there talking to him and he says he found a dog. I told him that the dog was mine as I had found him.

"First," he says, "you don't even know what dog I'm talking about."

I told him he was a red and white Kelpie with a studded collar and was full of cattle ticks and if he was no good, he's your dog. I had been up two or three times through the night to stoke the fire and had seen the dog then.

We packed up, saddled our horses and mustered the cattle and took them to the trucking yard. This dog did everything right. He was good at putting them into a mob and very good at forcing them in the yard. Guy Nanties came and gave us a hand to truck the mob and when we were ready to head back to Delillah.

I said to Guy to take Red, the dog, home and put him on a chain. That he did and when John and I got home, I dipped him for the ticks and wormed him as he was in very poor condition and sore footed. He had a job to walk on all fours.

The next week Guy sent John and me out to muster ewes out of the back paddock. I took Red with us because by this time he was fit and shiny. Johnny and I got on our horses at the gate and all you could see for a long way were sheep scattered in the open Gidgee country. All I did was point in towards the sheep and Red took off. He would go as far as he could see sheep and turn them in towards us. We mustered to a yard where we drafted them. This dog was unreal. He would work wherever you put him. When we had them in the forcing pens, he would get up on their backs and run along them and then come back through them and force them through the drafting race - there aren't many dogs that would do that. I told everybody that he even counted them on his own and, when they asked me how he could do that, I told them he would bark for every hundred and shit for every thousand! He wasn't that good but close to it.

I had Red for about six weeks when, one day, Guy came down to me at the horse yard where I was breaking in some horses and said that someone gave him a ring, asking if he had seen this dog. Guy asked me what would he tell this chap and I said, "No, that he didn't look after him. So tell him nothing."

That he did and, a couple of weeks later, Johnny and I went off to the Charleville races. I called Red to his chain but he didn't come. I said to John that I would leave him and tie him up when we came home that night. When we got home it was very late. I whistled Red and he still didn't come. I ended up going to bed and got up early. I went looking for Red and found him dead in the Warrego River. He died from eating the salvage off the sheep skin – we used to pour Coopers Dip on to the skins to stop the flies from blowing them and that's what killed one of the best dogs I ever had.

I finished at Delilah and went down to Kennersley, owned by the Nanties, a very nice family. Young Richard was a mechanic in the Air Force and was pretty good at tuning the Tigers 100 motor bike up. So, every time he knew I was going to town, he would tell me, "Bring your bike up and we'll have a look at it." He would tune it and then take it for a ride to test it.

I would leave early in the morning, go into Delilah and pick Monaghan up. He had an old single-pot Matchless, a heavy piece of shit. Every chance he got he would swap bikes. One morning, on our way in (we were in sandy country) I fell and his bike came on top of me. I wasn't hurt but the name-plate came around and I got a cut on my forehead and was bleeding. As I hit the ground I sang out. John heard me and he was trying to turn my bike around and, in sand, it's hard to do. I also had my swag tied on the back and that made it harder. I lay where I was, with my arm over the front wheel and it was still spinning and I was watching John. He thought I was hurt and was panicking.

When he finally got back to me and finished straightening and putting the bike back on the gip stand, I jumped up and said, "Boy, that was close!" When he saw that I wasn't hurt, did he go off and called me a few naughty names!

Sometime down the track, John got to know a lot of locals and you couldn't get him to go to Wyandra. But we did go to Wyandra one weekend and we met up with one of the local boys. He got the bright idea of putting on a dance in the local hall. He paid for the hall and band. We went and this poor bugger didn't even get one dance because he was too drunk.

I used to bike with the Castles as I was mates with Bobby and Benny; Ellen and Les were still going to school. I would get a job elsewhere if George didn't have any work. He mainly did droving locally and he was a good one at that. Had some good horses and dogs and if there was going to be any arguments, it would always be over who had the best dog or who owned what horse or who was the best rider.

Old George had a half breed dog called Jenny. He could do anything with her and she would never ever attempt to bite or kick him, no matter what – drunk or sober. I saw him one day, full as a fart, and he had Jenny tied up at the back of the Dalton Hotel and he was showing this bloke how quiet she was. He got down on all fours and was making out he was a dog and going through the motions of biting her on the back legs. Sent cold shivers up our spines. So Bob and I went down and got him away from the 'Jen' as she was known.

Every time I would go away, both Bobby and Ben would use my bike and one time I ended up in Brisbane, had a holiday and was going back. I was going to give the bike to Jimmy. So Big Joe, our brother-in-law to be, Jimmy and myself headed out to Charleville in Joe's little Morris Z ute. We drove all night and anyone who knows what or how big a Morris Z was would know that we had a very cramped ride. We gave Jimmy, who sat in the middle, heaps all the way.

They stayed at Castles and I headed out to Calgary Station to pick up my bike as Bobby was working with Terry Smith, fencing. I got back to town late and they decided that they would go to the pictures. I filled the bike up with petrol and I parked it over the bridge as it wasn't registered. After the movies we all headed home to Castles. We all got out of the ute and I went to start the bike. It flooded at the carby and when I gave it the boot it backfired and big panic, it caught alight.

Jimmy says to keep trying to start it and I said, "Frig it, let it burn." Jimmy rushed over and really tried to get it going but it had too good of a blaze.

So I said, "Throw it in the river." That's just what we did. You could smell the rubber burning for a long time after. We went back in the daylight, pulled it out of the Warrego River, dropped it off and Jimmy and Joe left to go back to Brisbane. I did get the bike going again but was windy of it after that.

I ended up going out to Rhonda Vale with a mate, Mickey Hackett, a good horseman - could ride a good bucker. He had 15 horses to break in as he was going to get a mob of Boatman cattle to go to NSW. So we ended up in Charleville town one weekend. Johnny came in and we got him drunk and instead of going home on Sunday, we kept him in town and over the weekend we talked him into leaving Guy Nanties on Delilah as we said he'd been there five years and that's all he knew, nothing else. We told him to come with us and we'd teach him to break in a horse and take him on the road droving. Johnny wasn't real sure and didn't know how to tell Guy. So I told him to take Mickey's car, a big black Chev.

"When you see Guy, and he will get up you, you just tell him you are leaving and give him a week's notice. And we will see you here next weekend."

John left us and Mick and I went about doing the horses and before long I looked up and said to Mickey, "That looks like your car coming."

Sure enough it was. John gets out all smiles and happy as anything. We ask him what happened and he tells us he met Guy at the horse paddock gate and Guy gets up him and says he can finish up now. Johnny knocks his arse in by telling him that he only came to get his gear as he had a job to go to, droving. It was a happy camp. We gave John a nice chestnut baldy mare and told him how to go about breaking it in. Over the next fortnight Mickey and I broke in 14 horses. They all rooted at one stage or another, all except the chestnut that John had because he spent that much time on her that she couldn't be anything else but quiet.

We got the wagonette and camp all set up and with the rest of the other horses, we left for Boatman. Mickey's uncle, Jimmy Hackett, had been doing the Boatman Station droving for years and was put on to manage it.

I was there with Mickey when Jimmy told him, "Mick, you have a 1,000 bullocks. That's what I want to see at the other end. And I also want to see six men at all time in your camp. Do the right thing and you will get all their work."

We started off on the trip of six weeks, the cattle going to a property in NSW called Midkin Station between Mungindi on the NSW border and Mooree. We had a cook, a big fellow, Dan Malone from Charleville, and two yellow fellows from anywhere, Big Frank, and Jimmy, Johnny, Mickey and me – six.

About 10 days into the trip, Mickey came to me and said he was going to hit Jimmy over the arse with the bridle and bush him. I advised him against it because of what his Uncle Jimmy said but Mickey reckoned he would never know. I said to Mickey that if he sacked Jim, Jimmy Hackett would be down the next day in his big Chev. Well, Mickey sacked Jim and put him on the mail truck to Cunnamulla.

Two nights later the cattle rushed (stampeded). They took a netting boundary fence and into a big paddock. We got most of them back on camp after a lot of galloping around. The next morning we counted the cattle and found we were 30 odd short. So Mickey has to send Big Frank back on his own and hopes that he finds them and then he has to catch us up. So he asked me if I would come back and give him a hand. So I said I would pack the wagonette with Dan, send him on by himself and I would put the plant horses with the cattle and do it that way.

We did just that and I was looking after the lead and the wing. Mickey stayed on the tail and part of the wing. We had the mob on a netting fence so it did make it a lot easier. We were going through scrub country so I kept the cattle just off the main road. Looking through the timbers I saw this car had stopped and a bloke was standing out from it. I rode over to him and sure enough it was the big man himself, Jimmy Hackett.

He says, "Gooday, how you going?"

"Good, Jim."

"You fellows have some trouble last night?"

"A little." I said.

"Where's Mick?"

"Back on the trail."

"Well, you go and tell him I will see him at the grid up the road."

I rode back to the train and there was Mickey, pushing them along and he was singing a cowboy song. Very happy until I told him who was waiting for him up front. He didn't believe me at first. Sometime later he came back to me very unhappy and he says that Jimmy knew all about the rush and how many he was missing. Told him that the owner of the property had helped Frank find them and that Frank was on his way. Says that he will see us early next morning as he was coming down to count the mob.

Frank caught us up on dinner camp so that afternoon Mickey wants to count the mob along a netting fence. Frank and me strung them out. I tallied for Mick while he counted them. He got 999 so then he got me to count them and I got 1,000. Not good enough so both Mick and myself counted them. I got 1,000 and he got 999 again. So we had a row and I said leave them as Jimmy was going to count them. The next morning Jimmy was back and he got on Johnny's horse. We strung them out and Mick says to Jimmy he would tally for him. Jimmy told him to string them along the fence.

When he finished counting them he rode up to where Mickey and I were, up at the lead and says to Mick, "There's 1,000 head there that I want to see at the other end. And you get another man out here as soon as you can and keep six men in the camp."

Everything went well until we got to Nindigully. That's a bit over half way. I came into the camp and everyone's around the fire having a heated discussion. Then Mick tells me he has just sacked Big Dan, the cook, over some silly thing. Dan had rolled his swag, got his cheque and walked over to the Nindigully pub so he was gone. Then Mick tells me he wants me to go cooking and he will put one of the darkies horse trailing with me. ext thing you know, Mick and I are having a big row.

"And what are you going to tell Jimmy when he finds out about it and turns up here?"

Mick says he's not worried and that Jimmy will never know.

I said, "Bullshit. I bet he knows about it already. Jimmy Hackett has been doing this for years, coming down this road and knows everybody along the way." And he did.

I said to Mick, "All he has to do is ring every one of these stations up and they would tell him how you're travelling."

The end of it was that I said to all of them, "I'll go cooking and Johnny can do the horse trailing as I will teach him and show him what to do. But the first bastard to complain about my cooking, he's it, he's the cook or I'll walk too."

Everyone agreed on that.

"And another thing, you won't be getting fresh bread and buns, jellies and cakes like you did with Dan."

That's what they did get from Dan. He was one of the best camp cooks that I had seen or heard of. Very cranky and we had a lot of rows that nobody knew of but I could handle him and we got on well.

I used to teal (knock off) two sheep every second day as the company wouldn't allow us to kill a beast but they would pay Mickey for all the meat he bought along the way. I would ride out of my way into places and ask the cockys for meat, to buy it, and they all knocked me back. Stupid thing to do. So all's I would do is ride out late in the afternoon with my little Smithfield bitch, called Bitch. She was a good one. We would muster a mob of sheep together, jump off my horse, grab a sheep and tie it down. While I was doing mine Bitch would grab a sheep and hold it down until I got to her. I never saw her get a poor one and she never, ever hurt the sheep.

After Dan left and I was doing the cooking, I would get up in the morning and cut the two sheep up (butcher them). I could butcher them properly but now I used to just cut through the back bone and I didn't care how I did it. Then I would cook them. The men would all sit around the fire eating and spitting out the small pieces of bone.

I would ask them, "How's the meat, boys?" And not one would complain. As Johnny said, they weren't game to. I would burn the custard, half cook the vermicelli puddings, do anything and nobody would complain.

Johnny did the horse trailing job well and we got on well together. We finished the trip and Mick paid us but owed me some and said he would fix me up when we got back to Charleville. He wanted me to take the empty plant back but I said no, so he and Johnny took it back.

Three of us, Big Frank Catey, Henry Gadd and myself, caught the old steam train from Thallon to Toowoomba and as that train went to Brisbane, we had to change at Toowoomba and catch another to Charleville. We left Thallon late in the day and arrived in Toowoomba early the next morning. We had been on the grog from the day before so we were still pretty tanked. The pubs in those days used to open their back doors around 6 am so we found one not far from the railway and started drinking for the day again.

Come 10 am we were running a bit short on money so I said to the two boys that we would go to the bank and cash our cheques. We tried all the banks in the main street but none would cash them for us, and even the pub where we had been doing most of our drinking wouldn't. We drank all day and we had to catch our train at 8 pm that night. I got into a fight with some coons in one pub and we got turfed out. That was all over that mob trying to get Frank and Henry to go to their humpys out at Harristown. They only wanted to get them out there so they could rob them.

We all had our cheques from Mickey for £120, a lot of money in those days. Wages were £14 and your keep per week. I lost my cheque in the pub, I think it was The Grand near the railway station. Somebody tried to cash it and the publican called the police. Big Frank and I were pretty pissed by this time and we headed back to the Grand looking for my cheque.

I was talking to the publican when the cop, he was a plain clothes cop, came in and sang out over the bar, "Hey Bourke. Out here." I ignored him and kept on talking to the publican.

Next thing, the cop came round, threw a £5 note on the bar, said to the boss that that was for the damage I had done having a bit of a punch up in the toilets and he wants me outside, now. On the footpath he gave me my cheque.

He said, "There's your cheque and there's your rail ticket. Your train leaves at eight pm, you be on it."

With that I snatched my cheque from him and said, "That's my money. The ticket, you can shove it and the train up your kyber because I'm not going." And walked off up to town.

Big Frank must have been watching me. I was on the main corner of Ruthlen Street and I asked three fellas for a match to light a cigarette and they told me politely to bugger off. I told them to go and get well f'd and Frank came and said, "The same goes for me." They looked at Frank and then me and they all took off.

Big Frank talked me into getting on the train and after I agreed to go, I stepped out on to the road and stopped a taxi. Frank got in the back seat and shouts out loud, "To the railway station mate and f'en quick."

We went straight in and were in our wagon and Henry says, "Did you get your swag and saddle from the storeroom?"

I said, "No, I'll go and get it." I got out and was walking alongside the train and the copper stood right in front of me and asked me nicely if I was going and I said no. He handed me my train ticket that I had forgotten about and said very firmly, "There's your ticket and there's your train." And tapped it, looked at his watch and said, "It leaves in three minutes, be on it."

With that I handed back my ticket, tapped the train and said, "There's my ticket, there's the train. I told you before what to do with them. Start from the train and work back with that."

He said, "If you're not going then you're going with me."

I told him he would need help. Next thing, his mate grabbed my arm from behind. Big Frank was going to be in it with me but I told him to get on the train as they wouldn't make it. Hard on him because he was a half caste.

"But just remember how I am, Frank." Was all the time I had. And as they marched me off the platform, one said to the other, "There's Big Jim." And nodded to him.

Only because I was drunk, I says, "Oh, scar face."

That's when they put the pressure on me. We got to their car, it was a Ford F100 ute, and the boss one says, "You look after him. I'll go check on the other two."

As he was pushing me in the front from the driver's side, he shoved me and pushed me on my back, pulled my shirt collar across my throat and with his short arm, started to punch into my throat. Every time he hit me I made out he was hurting me. He had me lying down on the seat and I was looking straight up at him.

Every time he hit me he would say, "Smart bastard, eh. Smart bastard from the bush."

Every time he said it I would say, "Yeah, smart bastard from the city. Get out you weak prick, I could put you through the roof."

With that he really got excited and got stuck into me. Punched the hell out of me around the head. Just then the No 1 came back from seeing Frank and Lenny off, he sang out, "Hey, hey, cut that out." And he stopped.

He said he would take me up to the lockup on his own as he was driving up. He says, 'Next time we tell you to get out of town, you'll go won't you?"

I was busy wiping the blood from my face and I said, "I'll see how smart you arseholes are in the morning."

"Yeah, and what are you going to do?"

I said, "My old man has friends in this town and one is a doctor and as soon as I am out that's where I'll be going and I have witnesses to say I never had a mark on me when you took me off the station. So go your friggin' hardest."

So he shut up and never said a thing until he got me inside. I had to take my boots and belt off and he was searching me. He was looking for my cheque again.

He said, "Where's your cheque?" I looked straight at him and said, "I've gone and lost it again. Now you go and find it again."

Straight away he slammed me against the wall, lifted his arm up and was going to punch me through that wall. The lockup sergeant sang out, "Hey, cut that out. He's in my care now and I don't want any more of that on him."

They locked me up for the night, cost me £1-10 and let me out at 6 am in the morning. While I was inside they had this other bushie in with me. He was broke and wanted a job and had nowhere to go. So I bailed him out and gave him my ticket to Charleville and told him who to see out there and I left him. I had enough cash left to catch a bus to Brisbane. I got out of the bus and caught a taxi to Bardon. When I got home, Mum and Pop were out. Lucky Kathleen was home. She gave me the cab fare, 5/-. I cashed Mickey's cheque and had a holiday with the family.

CAPTER NINE

I got back to Charleville some weeks later and I was nearly broke again so started to look for a job. You could get a job by just walking up town or out of any one of the pubs – and there were 10 of them. I was heading to the Charleville pub when I struck Mickey Hackett outside. He wanted to have a talk and a drink with me and I told him I wouldn't drink with him. We had a few heated words on the footpath. Everyone was looking at us. It was a Saturday morning and a lot of people were in town. He got me inside to the bar and he ordered two beers. I told him again I wouldn't drink with him and if he bought me a beer, I would spill it out. And that's exactly what I did. Mickey said that he had had a big row with his uncle, Jimmy Hackett, when he got back to Boatman Station. Jimmy said he would give Mick another chance and give him another mob. Mickey pleaded with me to go with him but I said no and told him what I thought of him. Said he could shove the money he owed me and walked away from him. He did do his next job and sometime later I heard that he had shot himself. I really felt for him because we had been mates for years on the Cooper. Did a lot of work together, rode a lot of mongrel horses. He was a good, rough rider in the mustering camps. It was sad to think he ended up the way he did. That was one droving trip I would never forget and I don't think Johnny Monaghan would either.

When Johnny and Mick got back to Charleville, they were in town and Johnny's old boss from Delilah, Guy Manties, came looking for him. He said his boss, Jimmy Nagel, who owned four other properties, asked Guy where the boy was, and Guy said he'd sacked him. Nagel told Guy to find John and to give him his job back or else. Johnny went back but didn't stay long.

There were two girls who came to Charleville. One was Leila Robinson. Her father was a painter. He had a big drop deck trailer, 40 footer, converted into a caravan pulled by an old Commer prime mover. And the other girl was Vi Redgrave.

Johnny cottoned onto Vi and he ended up marrying her. He worked around the district on properties. They had three kiddies – girl, boy, girl. The youngest got sick and by the time they got into town she was dead. She died in Vi's arms, in the car. They had a lot of trouble when they got to the hospital. When it was all over, they said the baby died from meningitis. They buried the girl in Charleville cemetery. They left the town and headed back to Brisbane and John ended up building a house next to his parent's place at Deacon. He got a job with his father, Frank. They had another daughter and some four or five years later, John rang me early to tell me that poor Vi had died in bed. He said she never gave him any sign, just passed away in her sleep beside him. It was very sad and a very sad funeral.

I stayed around Charleville working. I was breaking in horses and droving and ended up on Authoringa. Ashley Anderson was the manager, a nice bloke and good to work for. I was riding this bluey grey colt and Ashley told me to watch him as young Les Castles had been riding him and he used to gee him up a lot. Ashley told me he would root anytime of the day.

I was on my way home from a long day mustering. The horse was tired, so I thought. I got off at the horse paddock gate, rolled a smoke and went to get back on and the horse ducked his head and started to get fair dinkum. He threw me on to the pommel of the saddle and God, it hurt. I stopped him from rooting, got off and lit another cigarette. I had a spell, got back on, gave him a flogging, rode him home, let him go and thought no more of it. Three days later I was having a shower and felt a bit sore around my balls. I started feeling around and found I had three stones – wasn't a nice feeling. I put up with the pain for a couple of days but I got to the stage where I had a job to walk. So early one morning I slowly walked up to Ashley and told him what had happened. He said I better get on the wool truck and go to town and see a doctor.

That's what I did and I saw Dr Roper. He examined me then he started explaining things to me in big words and I didn't know what he was saying. As he was talking to me he was going through the pages of his big medicine book. He found the page he was looking for and he started talking to me in words I understood. I'll never forget the way he told me.

He said, "As you know there are six doctors in town. Any one of them can operate on you and wouldn't know what they were looking for. I'm retired, as you know, and I don't do any more operations. I have only seen two cases of this kind. One was a bookkeeper on a property and he was a bit heavier than you. I operated on him and he died. And you're the other one." Then he started talking about cancer and what happens down the track. I pulled out my cigs, lit one up and was puffing like mad. I think he was glad when I walked out of his office. A real nice doctor he was. He wrote me a letter for the Superintendent of the Brisbane General Hospital and advised me to go there and get fixed up and that I did. I saw a doctor, name of Courtis, a specialist. He did a good job on me. That was January 1958.

After I got over the op I went to Australia Estates in Creek Street and they got me a job on Terachi Station owned by Jackie Tully, a little blond lady and a tough little bushie too. It was about 90 miles out of Quilpie heading towards Windorah. I got off the mail truck buggered after the train trip there. I met the dirty old cook and a few of the boys and when I went for tea that's when I first met my wife to be – but didn't know of course. And boy, was she a honey.

We did the shearing muster and when that was done Miss Tully, got me to break in about eight horses and that's how I got to know Miss Susie Wilkinson who was the housemaid on the property. We took her out mustering and boy, that was something to see. This little one getting on a 17 hands high horse called Mickey. Then I took her around the paddock and taught her how to drive. That was a lot of fun. Both Sue and I left Terachi together on the mail truck. Old Jackie wished me well, said I could always get a job back there. Shook my hand, had a real good grip for a woman, as hard and a lot better than some men that I had met. She wasn't happy about Sue leaving but was quite nice, I thought, when she said goodbye. I think she knew we would be a couple. I have never, ever regretted that day.

More stories from the past …

One time with Old Alf Wheil on his property, Clarendon Station out on the Ilfracombe Road from Blackall, I very nearly walked on a big brown snake. This big fellow slides out of some turkey bush right in front of me. I heard him before I saw him. I kept my eyes on him while old Alf was looking for a stick. He was too slow so I jumped up a gidgee tree, broke off a dry short stick and killed the snake. We were saying how big he was, as in length and the width of his belly. As wide as a Tallyho cigarette paper which was two inches and that's wide for a shake's belly.

Old Alf says to me, "Paddy, I drew this block in 1931. It was very rough and scrubby in those early days. I have killed a lot of snakes since then but this fella is without a doubt the biggest I have seen and I have seen a few." I would say he was over seven foot or more long.

Another time I was in the shearing sheds with the Lindores brothers, Bob and Billy. We were shearing old Andrew Nickson's sheep across the Ballone River in St George, the Anchorage, but I am not sure of that. I had been there the year before and had done the shearing. The old fellow used to kill the sheep for the cook. This shearing, the boys refused to shear any sheep that had cancers on their ears and nose. There wasn't a lot, ½ dozen or more. The old fellow got cranky with the sharers over it but didn't say much. He met us at the gate as we were on our way to town. He thanked Old Bill and gave him £5 to shout the boys a drink.

So the next year it was the same gang did the shearing and when we were all in the truck again heading to town, he met us at the gate again. He gave Bill some money for the boys, thanked us and he asked if everything went well. Yes, yes, we all sing out.

Then he looks up at them and says, "Well you know them cancerous sheep you wouldn't shear for me last year?"

We all looked around at each other and answered, "Yes, Mr Nickson."

"Well," he said, "you ate the bastards this year." And with that said, he turned and walked away. That was the talk of the town for a while and something that I always remembered.

We were on the road near Thylungra Station on the Windorah Road, droving with this cowboy who married old Glen Martin's daughter, Joyce, a nice woman who knew more about droving than he did even though old Glen was a drover himself. He had a house in Quilpie town. This Charlie Bloomfield would always ride a piebald horse. He would ride on the road so when a car was coming in either direction, he would put the spurs into it. Of course, the horse would prance and short-step, move its head up and down and all the time Charlie would be holding the horse back. A real show-off so we nicknamed him Roy Rogers.

I remembered the day a bay horse bogged, laying down in the water hole. There was a pack saddle and bags on the bank of the creek. The mare wouldn't try to get up so, with the help of my cattle bitch and the whip, we got her up. She was carrying the kitchen sack because it was light and she was a light horse.

While I was on Springfield. My future brother-in-law, Bernie Biggs and this Keith Copp came out on the Winderah rail to work as musterers in the camp. That's where I had been some months and, because this station had just been sold, we were doing a general muster, drafting the fat bullocks off and handing them off to the drover in mobs of 500. Then the store bullocks in mobs of 1,000 and then the cows and calves in mobs of 1,000 or better. That was how we came to be on the road with this Roy Rogers character.

Our run was the last of the big musters and they were being held in a big holding paddock 20 miles down the road. The stock inspectors and a vet from Quilpie came out. We had the mob mustered and were tailing them out. They shot two cows at random, had a look at their lungs and whatever and declared that the whole lot had pleurisy. So the place was quarantined for six weeks I think it was. As they died, they would cut the ears off them, put the ears in a sugar bag and count them when they delivered their mob which was 1,000 odd. The boss got special permission to take the last mob of 1,200 to the trucks in Quilpie and straight to the meat works.

Back to Springfield ... When I first went there it was a good camp of seven. The head stockman was Tom Hackett, a good man to be with; taught me a lot. When I first met his brother, Micky Hackett, we became good mates from the start. The seven of us were: Neville Watson, who later went on to run the camp on Womblebank, out from Mitchell, Tom - arsehole and real crawler, Jerry Carter and three other fellows I can't remember and myself. So, when we went mustering, Tom always took me and Mick and Neville would take the other boys. We would leave camp in the dark and Tom and I would always be the last in, always just on dark. One night we came into the camp, took the saddles off, watered our horses and as we were leading them past the fire, the cook, who wasn't real bright, says to Tom, "I made damper today, Tom. What do you reckon?"

Tom and I could see it lying on a bag on the ground and it looked real big.

Tom says, "Yeah, it looks alright."

The next morning we have breakfast and cut our lunches using the cook's first damper, so we have corn beef and damper. As we met on a waterhole for dinner, we all boiled our quart pot and sat down to eat.

Tom was the first to spit his out. "Holy shit," he says. "What the hell have we here?"

Anyway, you couldn't eat the damper so when we got into camp Tom asked the cook, "What the 'f' did you put in that damper? It was high, yellow in colour and all cracked on the top. We couldn't see how it stayed in the camp oven anyway."

"Well," said the cook. "I made two. The first never turned out too good, I only put ½ cup of Aunt Mary's baking powder in that one so I made the other one and put a tin and ½ in that. How was it?"

The cook came on the mail last Sunday so Tom put him back on the mail the following Sunday. That's when Keith Copp came along and Tom put him on as camp cook and he was a good one.

We were all working up at the stockyards shoeing the camp horses and repairing the saddles and what needed fixing. Tom told Keith to take the wheelbarrow down to the store room and get whatever he needed. So he did.

When he came back Tom says, "Did you get everything you wanted?"

Keith says, "Yes but there's no tinned fruit."

"Why not?" asked Tom.

Keith says that the manager, Mark Wilkinson, was there and told him, no tinned fruit for the camp and made him put the tins back. Tom says to hold everything so we stopped work and went back to the bunkhouse. Half an hour later Tom comes up to us all sitting around the camp fire and says he gave Mark the option – no tinned fruit, no head stockman. We were all going to walk off with him but he wouldn't have it. He went to his room and wrote a letter to the next owners who had just bought Springfield Station. That was Jack White, and old Gidgee Whiskers, Bill Cameron. They owned Brunette Downs in the Territory and that's why we were doing the general muster. Tom gave Keith his letter and told him to give it to one of the new bosses who he said would be up pretty soon. So Tom left and we voted Neville Watson as head stockman.

We went out to do the final muster. We had to move quick as old Ben Williams, a drover, was bringing in the first mob of 1,000 bullocks off the train at Yaraka and we had to have ours ready for him to take them on to Quilpie. We had the last of the Springfield cattle at a holding place called Lulu. We drafted all the dry cattle off and turned the cows and calves bush. Neville left three boys to trail them out and yard them of a night so they got it easy. Neville, Mickey, Keith and me all went back to the head station to give Bill a hand to yard the mob and we had to run them all through the crush to inoculate them because they had pleurisy bad. They lost quite a few on that day. A big plane landed and the big boys arrived as Tom said they would. They were hanging around talking.

At the head of the crush, Keith said to me, "What do ya reckon?"

I said, "Go and give it to old Bill."

That he did. We were watching Bill read the letter, had a talk to Keith and then he called over Jack White. He read the letter, another talk and then they called Wilkinson over. We don't know what they said to him but they sure did have him moving around and shifting his fat. We all went down to the homestead and had dinner, then we came out to the plane. We were all looking it over when the big boys came with the pilot.

White says, "Well, boys. The pilot's here and he will take you all for a ride and show you the place from up there." We all looked at each other and none of us was game.

White says, "Well, boys, we can't hang around waiting any longer as this is costing us £600 an hour."

That's when he told us to stay on as things were going to change for the better. New quarters, better tucker and better facilities. With that they took off and we never saw them again. I was told that things did change. The best thing was they got rid of Mark Wilkinson.

That's when they got that special permit to move that mob of cows and cattle with pleurisy because they had been well clear of the in-coming cattle. So we all mustered the Springfield cattle and that's when the cowboy Charlie Bloomfield came out - was short of men and Keith Copps, Bennie Briggs and myself left Springfield. I had only been through it by car and couldn't believe what they had done – grids and good swinging iron gates.

We had a time in Quilpie. Keith had the shits with me over a fight we had on the way in. I don't know where he got to. Big Joe and I got a job on Mt Margaret out from Eromanga. The manager there was Charlie Weir, a little man. The pub manager was Jack Teen, Mary was his nickname, a real old woman. There were six jackaroos and two camps – one for the cattle and one for the sheep. So they put Joe and me into the sheep as they were shearing. We were there over a week and Joe said he would like to go down to the camp at the shearing shed as they got good tucker by the shearers. One day one of the jackaroos, Roger, wouldn't take his turn running the horses. So we all jack up.

Old Mary came out as usual and says, "What's the problem?"

I was the speaker and I told him that Roger was a bludger and didn't want to take his turn on the horses.

Old Mary looked at all of us, 10 in all, turned to Long Jim and says, "Jim, you run the horses." He was a roo and had to do what he was told.

Mary turned back to us and looked straight at Big Joe standing there with his arms folded and says, "Bernie, you roll your swag." And before he could say another word, Joe says, "I'm finishing up on the next mail."

Mary looked at me and I said, "That goes for me too."

Old Mary had his hands on his knees, he straightened up and says, "Alright. Well, Bernie, you still roll your swag and you can finish your time down at the shearing shed."

As we walked away Joe says, "Shit, I thought he was going to sack me."

So that was a short stay but at Mt Margaret it was known for going through the men. They had a three way with men – one coming, one going and one staying. A shit place and bad tucker.

We went back to Quilpie and Hughie McHugh wanted two men. He was coming in with a mob of 500 fat bullocks from Nockatunga, going to the meat works at Bourke, NSW. That was a good trip, plenty of food and water and quiet cattle. It was good till we got to Yantabulla, NSW. There was a common and seeing as we had travelled nearly 200 miles you were allowed to spell for two days. It was raining and we were all wet and cold. So Hughie let the cattle go and we got on the grog. Had a good night drinking 30% plus proof Red Mill Rum.

The next day we had it easy and got on the grog again. That afternoon I was out hobbling the horses when Joe comes out of nowhere and says we were finished. Hughie pulled the whip on Joe, silly thing for Hughie to do, but Joe took it off him. He told Hughie he was finished and so is Paddy. So it was the first time that I finished a job and had no say in it.

We went back to Quilpie and Joe took off, back home I think, and I got a job on Congie. Hughie Tully was the owner and one of the best places and man that I worked for. He put me on horse breaking at £5 a head and station wages plus 5/- a shoe if I shod them, which I did, and that was good money in those days.

Hughie got me to see him every morning and tell him what horse I was working on. He would look up his horse book and tell me that one will buck or rare or bolt and that's exactly what it would do. So I was always pre-warned so to speak. Les Betters from Quilpie was the head stockman and a good one. He had his young son, Johnny, there with him. I asked Les if I could put Johnny on some of the young colts and he said yes, but not to put him on anything rough.

Hughie Tully was a polo player and looked it. So Johnny and I would get on his playing field with his polo bats and balls and we would push each other around - really made some of the young colts.

We drafted the bullocks off for the rodeo in Eromanga and boy, they were spikey. Hughie was on the committee and said he was finding it hard to get riders. The day came and I went into the rodeo and I walked over to the yards to have a look at the horses buck. I watched only two, the first was off just out the shute, the next came out holding on to the monkey so his mate in the crown yelled out to him, "Hook him, Joe."

Joe screamed back, "I can't, I can't."

With that I walked back to the pub. I passed Hughie on the way back and I said, "Bloody awful, Hughie,"

He said, "I know Paddy, but we have to give him a go."

Sometime later this loud mouth comes to the bar all excited and saying out loud, "I won, I won!"

Mr Tully had given me a job on his property. The loud mouth didn't know that I was working there and I said to him I heard he had some rough horses to ride and he says, "I don't care, I'll ride 'em."

About a week later, Les says, "Paddy, grab the jeep and head over to Pinkilla and pick up a man off the mail."

I took Johnny with me as the gate opener. When we got there and I saw the loud mouth, I said to Johnny, "Don't let him in the front and don't give him the gun."

Hughie had a new .222 with a scope and a good one. On the way back all Loud Mouth wanted to do was get in the front and have a chat and I wouldn't let him and that really pissed him off. He did get a shock when he first saw me. Unfortunately, the only bed left was in my room. All he could do on the Sunday was brag about how good he could ride.

So on the Monday morning as we were walking to breakfast, Les says to me. "You can hand the horses out, Paddy, and if you haven't got something to shut him up, I have. He's got a tongue as long as Johnny's hair." And it was long.

When we got back to the yards I had all the young horses drafted and there was these two really good looking ones. One was black with white marking and the other was a nice chestnut with white markings. I said to Loud Mouth, "Take your pick."

He says, "I'll take that one." Pointing to the chestnut .

I said, "No you won't. You take the black and stick your hand out on him and see how you go."

The black was snorty and ready to fire. I had to catch him and I saddled him also. All my horses that I break in will stand still and quiet while you get on them and what happens once you get on is up to them. This black could buck pretty high. I told Loud Mouth to ride him in the round yard.

As he was leading him in he asked me, "What's he like?"

I said, "Stick your hand on him and he will see how good you are."

I said to young Johnny, "Get up on the rail and make sure he gets his off side stirrup iron."

The horse takes two steps and starts to buck. Loud Mouth went up in the air and came down and landed flat on his guts. The horse was still bucking and roaring beside him.

I sang out to Johnny, "Quick, open the gate." And he did.

The horse took off bucking with the saddle, like they do. I got Loud Mouth up and saw him right. Then Hughie Tully came up to me and said, "What are you going to do, Paddy? Let him go or what?"

I said, "No, I will have to take it out of him."

I took the horse outside, got a bit of No. 8 fencing wire, three foot long and twisted it. I told Hughie that this was cruel but he needs it now. So I got on top and Les Betters handed me the wire and I took him off. Straight away he started bucking and every time he went up I laid into him with the wire and every time I hit him I sang out at him. He finished rooting and took off down the paddock. I bought him back and had to talk Loud Mouth into riding him. After the hiding I gave him, the horse was alright and was a lovely horse to ride.

Three days later I had to go down to the shearing shed where they were mustering for the shearing as the black had thrown Loud Mouth. The horse had bucked him off again, then bolted and went through a barb wire fence and cut himself about a bit. I got on him and he took off rooting. All the shearers came out to watch me ride him. I backed into a big box tree and took my foot out of my side iron. I landed on my ass and put my hand out as I hit the ground and there right beside me was a broken beer bottle. That turned me cold. I got old Pat the cowboy to ride a quiet hose back with me and all he wanted to do was play up. Anyway, Hughie sacked Loud Mouth.

Congie Station would have been one of the best stations that I worked on and I had been on quite a few. I knew all the Tullys around Quilpie and without a doubt, Hughie was the best. Then came Joe and then Jackie, Cameron, Paul, and Jack. Ray you wouldn't talk to.

It was Christmas day and big Joe Briggs and me had 500 fats on the bore drain that runs through Naretha Station – that's Cameron Tully's place. It was stinking hot. We had the meat bag full hanging from a gidyea tree and smoke fires going because of the flies. We were told by Hughie McHugh, the boss, to hold the mob there until he caught up. He went back for a few head that we had missed. It was about midday when along comes Cameron in his flash ute and started going off about us camping where we were and told us to get moving or he would move us. And with that we got into him and with a few chosen words told him where he could go and he did. He couldn't move us on because we were on the stock route and it was ½ mile wide and many miles long.

CHAPTER TEN

Sue and I got married down at Redcliffe in the Congregational Church. We were married by Bonnie's cousin Tom, nice sort of bloke but was a bit pissed off with me because I was a little drunk. Not much but enough to be a bit happy! Brother Tom and Barrie put on a small spread for us and it was only my immediate family.

Sue and I had a green Zephyr 6 sedan, a good car. It had a bad shudder in the motor – a broken gear-box mount. So I fixed it outside Tommy's place in Sutton Street. After the party it was dark and Sue and I were ready to go. I was taking Sue back to Les and Linda's place at Mitchelton. They all put Sue in the front and they walked me around the back, all pushing me, laughing and going on silly. They pushed me in the seat and said see ya later. It would have been around 8 pm or more. Sue said she wanted a Sunday Split – it was the thing in those days. We drove right to the top of Queen Street and I had to back into this car spot, no parking metres then. The trams were running both ways and then I saw everybody looking. When I got out and walked around to the footpath, some old fellow happily came up to me. He was a new Aussie so I had a job to understand him.

"What's this, a big joke?" he says.

I was about to piss him off until he took me around to the back of the car and, laughing, he said, "What's this?" and pointed to this string of old shoes. I don't know how many but they were all over the back. They had the usual Just Married – I think it was written with Tommy's shaving cream. I took one look under the shoes, left them there, jumped in the car and said to Sue, "No ice cream tonight. I'm getting out of here."

We went to Les', stayed there the night, and I left my lovely Sue at four in the morning, headed to Inala and picked big Joe Bernie up and we headed for Moree. Sue stayed in on Brisbane for a few months helping out with my family.

We didn't make it and boy, what a trip! On the way I blew a tyre on the back on top of the gap, south of Warwick. Poor old Joe he wasn't feeling too good from the night before. No jack, so we looked around and found a big rock. I pulled out a long strainer from the fence and, with that and the rock I lifted the car while Joe changed the wheel. Off we go again and Joe was driving now. We used to sit on 100 miles an hour or more

– the Zephyr could do 130 miles an hour easy and used to corner real well.

We got just this side of Bonshaw, on the Inverell Road and Joe gets another blow-out. I was running on retreads – good for around town but no good on the bush roads, nearly all dirt in those days. Well, the look on old Joe's face! I can still see the sad look of despair.

"Old Joe, what are we going to do now? No money and no more bloody wheels. What are we going to do?" I couldn't stop laughing at him.

Here he was, this big, strong bastard, really down. We had knocked around, travelled a lot of miles together, never ever had a lot of money, made a lot but spent it, drank it. I did, anyway. And here he was, lost. Well, there was a cocky across the road and he was drenching a mob of his sheep in his old set of yards.

I said, "Come on, we'll see if will give us a job." We walked up to him and I told him that we have a job to go to in Moree (we didn't) but we had run out of tyres. "Can you give us a job?"

I thought we had won him but he changed and said, "No."

So I asked him, "Could I leave the car there for a week or two?"

He said, "Yes."

So we walked back and I drove the car on a flat tyre, parked it under a big willow tree and set off hitchhiking to Moree. We got there late that night. The next day some man that Joe knew got us a job putting a roof back over a big wheat stack. In those days wheat was all in bags. We made good money, then, but it only lasted the week. On that weekend I went to a garage in South Mooree and bought a second-hand tyre, a 13" for 30 bob, £1-10.

He said, "Take that one, mate. It'll get you out of trouble." It turned out one of the best second-hand tyres I ever bought – I couldn't wear it out.

I left Joe after work and said, "I'll see you when I see you." I took the tyre and tube and the old-type hand pump. I got a lift by a truckie to Inverell. Walked from town to the outskirts, stopped on a bend under a street light, pumped the tyre up with the pump. My thinking was they would see the tyre, pump and me. I was clean and tidy. It was dark when this ute pulls up. It had four adults in the front and nothing in the back. They were all pissed, laughing and going on.

The driver was bent over the wheel and he says in broken English, "You want lift?"

"Yea, mate, I'm going to Bonshaw."

"So are we," he says, "but no room in front."

He pointed to plenty in the back so I quickly threw everything in and sat on the passenger side, right in the back corner. The road was very narrow bitumen, enough for one car and no more. All roads were the same then. I could hear and see them drinking. He was poking along about 50 miles an hour and I was quite happy until this sedan comes up from behind, heading the same way. But he was really flying. It didn't worry me until he got beside us and was going to overtake. The next thing they were cooing and yelling, laughing and the ute was staying with him. The bloke in the sedan worked it out – he put his foot down and, boy, he was moving. He was on the side in the dirt and, when he got in front, we slowed right back to what we were doing before. I could see the lights of Bonshaw coming and then another car coming up on us. All I could say to myself was, God, mate, stay back. He slowed down, waiting for him to catch up. But we came into town and he pulled up outside the pub. They fell out, staggered round and they invited me in to have a drink. To do the proper thing, I went in to shout for them but they wouldn't let me shout. I was at the bar, talking to one of the locals while they were around the other side of the bar and everyone was laughing and joking, patting and kissing the lady that was with them.

I was telling this local what he had done out on the highway, frightening the shit out of me. "Bloody mad," I said.

Then he told me that they had just come from burying their two-year old son who had swallowed kerosene. He said, "They're not like us. They celebrate. That's why they're so happy." And I could understand then what it was all about. Really nice lot of people.

I walked out to my car, fixed it and was back at Mooree at daylight. What a day! What a trip!

Joe went back to Brisbane and, after a week of pulling burrs, I got a job running the dairy for old George Mills – the only dairy around that district. I milked 72 cows morning and afternoon. He couldn't get enough milk so he used to buy it in and Max, his son, who had the milk run, would pick it up from the rail.

Sue eventually came out from Brisbane and joined me on the station. I used to bring her up to the dairy in the afternoon and we used to crimp and put the milk in all the cartons. She liked it.

We were living in a bus in the council park and, boy, was it hot! Also, when it rained, the bus would leak everywhere. I tried hard to get a flat to live in in town but to no avail. That's when I went out to Midkin Station on the Mungindie Mooree Road and got a job boundary riding. No furniture, just the Zephyr sedan – we were paying that off at £5 a week and it kept us broke. We never had enough money to do anything or go anywhere. Poor old Sue never complained once.

SUE'S STORY

I first met Paddy at Terachi Station where I was employed as a housemaid. The owner was Miss Jackie Tully and her sister was Evelyn. The old cook, Mrs Ryan, was not a very clean woman. Then there was Old Alex - he had only one eye. Old Joe was the Aboriginal man – very friendly but he didn't do very much around the place. I was employed as the housemaid.

One day the mailman drove in and this young, tall, thin man jumped out of the truck - Paddy Bourke.

After dinner at night, we used to sit out on the kitchen steps and chat and Paddy would tell me about his droving trips. Miss Tully used to let me go with her and the men to muster up cattle and sheep. Paddy said I was very lucky because most of the housemaids were not allowed to have anything to do with the ringers.

Paddy also took me for a couple of driving lessons but Miss Tully did not like it. She said I was too young - I was 17 years old then.

After a month or so Paddy left and went on a droving trip for a month or so. He wrote me a lovely letter though.

Then I was told Paddy had gotten into a big fight and could have gone to jail. Miss Tully put a good word in for him and he came back out to our station to break in a couple of horses. By then I had turned 18.

Paddy had to go down to Brisbane as he and his brother had brought their parents a new home. He asked me if I would go with him and I said yes. Of course, Miss Tully wasn't very happy about it. Housemaids were hard to find in the outback and she didn't want me to leave.

After that we got a job on Clonard Station on the Cullamara Road. Lovely small cottage and I did a little housework. We were there quite a few months. We went into town and stayed at a small hotel. We then found out Jack Kerbie didn't sign Paddy's cheque but luckily he had signed mine. We cashed mine at the hotel and it paid for our food and drinks. It was the weekend and no banks were open and because we didn't want to stay until Monday, we did a 'daylight flitter'. After that we were married and went from station to station.

We got a job at Blackall Lighthouse Station and by then we had our first son, Stephen, who was still a baby. We had a long trip to get to Blackall, plus a broken windscreen to fix. Ted Crowhurst was the manager and not a very nice one at that.

So we pulled up at a small creek to wash up before meeting the boss. But he just pulled up behind us and had a talk to Paddy. When Paddy got back into the car he said, "Don't unpack too much as we won't be long here. We'll just get enough money and be off."

Paddy was talking to a Jack Hoff who was owner of quite a few thousand acres. Paddy told him about Ted and how bad he was and told Jack he was going to kick Ted up the ass and if Ted tells the police he'll have to pull his pants down to show them. Somehow word got around and Ted Crowhurst was a much nicer man after that.

We were there nearly four years and had two boys by then. After that we came to Brisbane and bought our first home. Paddy then worked for his mate, Jim, on house stumpings but only for a couple of years as they went bust.

He then got into removing people's homes for a couple of years. He brought his own plate top truck and then went into a prime mover truck and trailer. By then we only had the two youngest at school and Paddy wanted to go out bush again. So we went to Charlevelle – Old Buss McCain's Gumdare Station.

We stayed there four months then Paddy's father died so we came home again and waited for the two youngest to finish school and get jobs.

We then went out to Roma to Muldoon Station owned by Alister Bassingthwaite. The cottage was one big mess. No furniture and what was there was 200 years old but he gave us a bed - old, and a new kitchen sink with no plumbing. We were there for one month and it was three hours into Charleville or two hours to Roma. So again, we came back home. But by then Paddy didn't have good health - he got a germ in the blood.

We bought a house out Blacksoil with 62 acres. We got a few poddy calves and a couple of horses. We built a four car shed and it fell on Paddy, breaking his back. When his back mended, Paddy would do small jobs out west with a mate, Darrell, while I stayed at home.

THE FINAL ADVENTURE

In 2006, after 46 years of marriage, Sue and I went out bush again to see if things had changed but they hadn't. I got a job caretaking on Muldoon Station, Mungallala. The property was 90 km north of the now dead town of Mungallala. It used to be good to stop at. I was young when I was working around the area and I would always buy their stores and have a bit of a drink at the pub, the one and only and still is the only pub right on the highway.

Sue and I left home at Brassall on Sunday morning, early, and headed on out. We only took the bare essentials. We got to Munga around midday and met the boss. I had told him what I was driving, a white Holen ute with a canopy cover and registration number. I rang him at Wallumbilla as that's where his property, Younga Burga, was. He told me to carry on and he would meet me at Mungallala. So we did and I saw two four wheel drives coming up on me between Mitchell and Mungallala.

I said to Sue, "I bet that's him in one of those," when they flew past us.

We got into Mungallala a bit after 12 pm and we waited for ½ hour, on the side of the main road so as he could see us. I was about to go to the pub when sure enough, one of those utes 4 x 4 came past us and he stopped. It was Alistair Bassingthwaite. He had a bit of a yarn and he asked me what speed I travelled at and I said I had the cook with me so not too fast, around 70 to 80 kph. Well, he took off and rarely got under 85. When we finally got to Muldoon Sue was happy as the trip was wet and too fast for her.

The first words Old Bass, as he was called, said when we got out was, "Well, that's your cottage and that's mine over there. It's a bit rough but I am going to put cladding on it in about two weeks' time, when I get the carpenter out."

I told him the appearance didn't worry us. So we walked into the house yard, up to the back door and boy, was it a mess. He apologised and said he was going to get the boys to clean it up and carried on with more bullshit. He walked us through and turned the fridge on, it would have been as old as him, 64, but it went.

We went through to the main bedroom and there was only an old cupboard, no bed and Sue said, Where's the bed?"

He said, "You have no furniture?"

"No," Sue said.

He said he would get us one from his cottage. We all went over to his old cottage and it's as dirty as ours. He looked at Sue and asked what sort of bed she wanted and he was looking at two old farm gates, which is what we called them 30 years ago.

Sue told him straight, "We've been married for 46 years and never slept in single beds." So he said we could have his, a small old double. We took it over and set it up but Sue said she would clean it down before we put the mattress on. It was as old as the bed.

He wanted to show me the waters and he was in a hurry as he was leaving to go to Tambo, a good three hours or more drive. He drove around the paddocks in his new 4 wheel station wagon, had all the good gear in it. I ended up sick and he had to wait for me to have a chunda. So he cut the tour short and headed back home where we had a yarn and agreed on a few things. Then he went and saw Sue who was busy cleaning out the cottage, said hooray and was gone.

Sue had swept all the chook shit, mice shit and everything else out the back door. We unpacked, made the clean bed up and we had our first meal that night. The tank water was rusty and dirty but we had bore water which was pretty good to drink but when we saw the tanks that it came from, I said to Sue, "I think we'll use the rain water." So what we did was run the tap until it cleared up.

We had two chairs to sit on, a good size table, a sideboard - old, and a kitchen cabinet - very old with no door on it at all. The sink fell apart and he had to replace it for $500. He told me it would have been there when they shifted the cottage from the neighbour's property.

Bass told me that when he and his father first bought Muldoon in 1956, he was a boy of 16 years. While we were putting the new sink and cupboard in, I said, "You going to have a cup of tea?"

He said, "No thanks. I never stop for a cup of tea."

I said, "Well, Sue has made it."

"Righto," he says.

He sat down and we had a yarn about everything. Then came dinner time. Sue had sandwiches made for all. He came in with his bag, pulled out his lunch and Sue says, "I have these."

He says, "Oh, okay. I had these from yesterday so I will keep them for tomorrow." He wrapped them back up, put them away and ate Sue's. He turned out quite a nice bloke to talk to but boy, was he tight.

The following week he came back and when we were having a cup of tea, Sue asked him, "Did you have your sandwiches the next day?"

Alistair said, "Oh, yes. It was alright." Sue couldn't get over that.

The time came we had to go to town to get groceries. We leave the place at 5.45 in the morning and we decided to go to Charleville instead of Roma - both are about the same distance. We pulled up at our friend's, Ellen Pugsley's, place at 9.15 am nearly 3 ½ hours travelling and it was hot, 40°C in the shade. Everyone was saying how hot it was. We did our shopping and had dinner with Ellen at the Charleville Hotel. Then we went back to Ellen's and had a yarn and a cuppa and left just on 3 pm. We got back to Muldoon a bit after 6 pm. Sue was buggered as it took us 12 hours to go to town just to get our tucker. That's when I decided we would not be staying there. Sue wasn't happy as she missed the grandkids. Only because the girls were ringing her in turns at night did Sue stay there, otherwise she would have walked out.

I went down to the bore head early morning to pump water up to the house and for the cattle and as I walked through the gates I nearly walked on this big, shiny, coppery brown snake. I got a hell of a fright. I stepped back quick and grabbed a stick I had at the gate for that purpose and I came at him from the side. He was trying to get into the long grass. I up him with the stick that was five foot long and he started to flatten out and hiss real loud. The stick started to break each time I hit it and ended up real short, about 18 inches long. I got him and I said to Sue if he had bitten me, I would have been dead or near to it by the time I got back to the cottage. So I was very cautious after that and never saw any other snakes, but they would have been there.

All the kids came out for the weekend and that was lovely to see and have them there, even for a short time. But we had had enough. So the first opportunity I got I told Alistair we would be going. He wasn't happy with me so I said I would wait until he got another man or until Thursday week – another wrong move.

The kids left and that was upsetting for Sue and me but the men came and they started mustering for the branding and that gave me something to do. I don't know how many calves they branded but when you saw them spread out in the paddocks there seemed a lot. They had 4,000 head on 36,000 acres. Had good fences going back a few miles. Good water and plenty of it. He had three sub bores but one had collapsed and so it wasn't in use. That was on Snake Hill. One was sucking a bit of air which I bought to his attention but he wasn't concerned about it.

Alistair was always coming and going so it was hard to catch him and have a talk to. I would have liked to have told him that if he put in a bit of furniture and gave me, or anybody else, some extra like the phone or tucker – a bit of meat, he might keep the good ones that come along. But for what he paid, $100 a week and for where it's at, 3¼ hours to town, nearly 300 km, to me it wasn't worth the effort. But we do admit that he did try to make us comfy. Gave us a good freezer, two comfy lounge chairs, the two original kitchen chairs we had I chucked in the dump. And the two beds he was going to give Sue and I to sleep on I chucked in the dump – he told me to.

THE FINAL WORD

Our life in the droving and station work years were very good and we were very happy. The life was a lot freer, more relaxed and less tense than living in the city. We made lots of very good friends.

If we had been able to educate our children in the outback on the various stations we would have stayed in that lifestyle. But instead, they would have had to go to boarding school and we didn't want that, so we moved into Brisbane so they could attend school.

We will always look back on those years as the best years of our lives.

Paddy and Sue Bourke

Paddy, Sue and baby Stephen at Blackall

www.ingramcontent.com/pod-product-compliance
Lightning Source LLC
Chambersburg PA
CBHW050543300426
44113CB00012B/2241